DATE DUE			

LOUISIANA STATE UNIVERSITY STUDIES
Max Goodrich, General Editor

Humanities Series
Donald E. Stanford, Editor

Number Fourteen
The Literary Career of Maurice Thompson

THE LITERARY CAREER
OF
MAURICE THOMPSON

by
OTIS B. WHEELER

LOUISIANA STATE UNIVERSITY PRESS

BATON ROUGE

MCMLXV

FOREWORD

IT WOULD BE impossible in a single phrase to characterize a man like Maurice Thompson. Engineer, lawyer, politician, scientist, poet, novelist, critic—to many of his contemporaries he was an adept in all of these fields, almost a universal genius. To other of his contemporaries he was simply the gadfly of the literary journals: a voluble, perverse, and irritating man, for his was one of the loudest voices in the "genteel" reaction to realism during the last fifteen years of the nineteenth century. In these extremes of opinion lies one reason for this study. It is unlikely that both sides were wholly deceived, but at the same time it may be that each faction represents only a partial view.

The other reason lies in the tendency of American literary historians in the twentieth century to give first attention (and rightly so) to the writers who determined, or perhaps divined, the direction in which American literature was moving. The feeling has been that men like Mark Twain, William Dean Howells, and Henry James were more significant than their popular contemporaries who have been even more completely overruled than they in the court of time. Of course this is true. Any generation must, for obvious reasons, see more significance in those writers of a previous generation who have in some way pointed the line of future development. It is also true that Twain, Howells, and

James have better survived the test of time because they were artists of a finer grain than most of their popular contemporaries. However, the ranking artists of a period by no means fill the literary scene; they may, in fact, be less representative of that scene than some of the lesser lights. Thompson's work, I believe, is an excellent index to the real temper and quality of American literature from 1875 to 1900, or rather to that larger part of it that we call genteel.

In my research and writing I have received much help, which I have tried to acknowledge in the footnotes. This has not always been possible, so I should like to express here my obligations to my wife for her forbearance and for her help, professional, clerical, and financial; to Professor Theodore Hornberger, who first suggested the topic and offered many helpful suggestions in the writing; to Mr. Frank E. Davis, who generously enabled me to examine the Thompson books, manuscripts, and personalia belonging to the estate of his late wife, Josephine Ballard Davis, Thompson's granddaughter; and to the Louisiana State University Council on Research, for a grant which enabled me to complete the work.

In the interests of both brevity and stylistic ease I have referred to several magazines by abbreviated titles which the following table will explain:

Lippincott's	*Lippincott's Monthly Magazine*
Scribner's	*Scribner's Monthly*
Critic	*The Critic and Good Literature*
Harper's	*The Harper's New Monthly Magazine*
Appleton's	*Appleton's Journal*
Scott's	*Scott's Monthly Magazine*

To append a bibliography would be pointless since the publication of Dorothy R. Russo and Thelma L. Sullivan's *Bibliographical Studies of Seven Authors of Crawfordsville, Indiana* (Indianapolis, 1952). The detailed Thompson bibliography in their volume has served me as an invaluable reference tool.

Finally, a note on diction. The area we know as the Midwest was known to Thompson and his contemporaries as the West. I have not attempted to change Thompson's diction in quotations and summaries, but in my own comments I have observed present usage.

O.B.W.

CONTENTS

The Literary Career of Maurice Thompson

CHAPTER I

THE MAN

IN HIS MATURITY, Maurice Thompson wrote of a boyhood experience which epitomized many qualities he admired. His account, for one seeking the roots of his sensibility, presents a symbolic tableau. Both the choice of detail and the perspective suggested by diction and tone reveal his commitment to what we have come to regard as a stereotype of "Old South" society.

The setting is a farmstead in the Cherokee hills of northwest Georgia. Picture a slim, dark, hazel-eyed boy, possibly twelve or thirteen, crawling under a gap in a thorn hedge, there to lie on the early summer grass in rapt admiration while he watches a splendid procession from the rich Georgia middle plateau wind along the road in front of his father's upland plantation house. It is a planter and his family going to their summer home deep in the hills. First comes a barouche drawn by a pair of dappled grays, driven by a grave black coachman in white gloves and polished boots, and carrying a dignified man of military aspect, with his "noble-looking" wife and dessicated spinster sister. Next passes a barouchet, drawn by a span of white ponies and bearing the young ladies of the family who, sporting demurely, smile faintly at the intense boy in a way that he will not forget. Behind the barouchet, on spirited horses, ride the two stalwart sons, darkly handsome, decorous enough, but betraying by a certain set of mouth and eyebrow a predilection to passion and violence, capable of folly or heroism depending upon the stimulus and the situation. Mule wagons filled with trunks and gabbling servants bring up the rear.[1]

To the boy then, as to the man later, this was a glimpse into an immensely desirable world. And to the boy it was a not altogether unattainable world, for he was the son of a moderately prosperous yeoman farmer and could therefore aspire to something better than could the sons of poor whites or "crackers," or slaves, among whom his own family was accounted gentry of a sort. Indeed, his aspirations could go beyond those of most farmers' sons, for his father was also a minister of the Gospel, a preacher of the Primitive Baptist faith, as was his father before him. His mother, too, was of a different stamp than most of the women who presided over the meager domestic establishments of the hill farms. In the roomy log house were bookshelves which she had filled with volumes of the English poets, the French, Latin, and Greek classics, and the works of Scott. So it was not only from occasional glimpses of the aristocratic life of the nearby area that the boy's aspirations toward the gracious, the heroic, and the noble were fed; he was also a familiar of Sir Philip Sidney and the Knight Ivanhoe and the Lady Rowena. And as he himself was to say many times in later life in defense of the values of gentility and in opposition to the values portrayed by a rising generation of rebels in fiction, "We grow like what we contemplate."

But these influences only begin to explain the highly complex sensibility that is reflected in the mature work of Maurice Thompson. Perhaps this sensibility is not to be explained entirely by biographical data, but they help. Certainly one important factor is his ancestry. Through both his mother and father he was descended from colonial families. His mother's maiden name was Diantha Jaegger. She was born in 1813 in New York State of Dutch ancestry, the daughter of a soldier in the War of 1812 who moved to Indiana in 1818. The family must have been of some means because she was given a rather unusual education for a woman of that period: she was able to direct the early education of her sons with the help of only an occasional tutor for foreign languages and mathematics.[2] Both her interest in educating her sons and the disabilities under which she worked are indicated by a note made by Thompson on the title page of his father's hymnbook: "Out of this book, at my Mother's knee, when but two years old, I learned my a, b, c's by the capital letters beginning the hymns."[3]

A good clue to the quality of the paternal influence is supplied by the autobiography of Maurice Thompson's grandfather, Wilson

Thompson.[4] Here the family is described as blending English, Welsh, German, and Scottish blood, the earliest identifiable forebear being a certain Closs (Klaus) Thompson who moved his clan from North Carolina out into the new land of Kentucky in 1787. His son, Closs, Jr., was the father of Wilson Thompson, who was born in Woodford County, Kentucky, a short distance to the west of Lexington. The autobiography, surprisingly similar in tone and content to that of the Methodist circuit rider Peter Cartwright, reveals a fervid, forceful personality driven by a sense of utter dedication. Those were the days when the principal requisite for being a preacher on the frontier was the "call." The agonizing doubts through which Wilson Thompson passed before being sure of the call made his commitment all the stronger when it came. And throughout a long life this almost messianic feeling never weakened.

Wilson Thompson married in Kentucky, moved to the vicinity of Lebanon, Ohio, and thence on to southeastern Missouri, where Maurice's father, Grigg Matthew Thompson, was born in 1811. But shortly after this the Thompson family settled in the White-water country of eastern Indiana, at this time a region peculiarly rich in political and intellectual activity. The town of Brookville, on the Whitewater River, furnished between 1816 and 1840 two U.S. Senators, three governors of Indiana, two justices of the state supreme court, and one representative to Congress.[5] A man of commanding aspect, Wilson Thompson quite ·naturally drifted into politics, serving one term in the state legislature during the 1820's and later being defeated for Congress by only a few votes. But preaching was his forte, and throughout his long life he was a pulpit figure of wide reputation and genuine power. His grandson recalled seeing him preach at the age of seventy-two: "He was straight, broad-shouldered, deep-chested, lion-faced; and his voice might have jarred and tumbled the walls of Jericho."[6] Another story recounts that, at a camp meeting in an Indiana maple grove, he once held the rapt attention of an audience of between seven and eight thousand for only a few minutes less than three hours. It was a period of doctrinal controversy, particularly between the Methodists and the Baptists, and Wilson Thompson, despite his lack of formal education, wrote a substantial amount of polemic literature.[7] On the whole he seems to have been a member of that legendary race of giants, of whom Peter Cartwright was the prototype, who subdued the wilderness, rifle in one hand and Bible in the other, gaining strength from their piety and piety from their strength. At least he seemed so in his grandson's eyes, and it would be the concept rather than the actuality that influenced the grandson's development. The stories that the boy Maurice heard at his grandfather's knee and his recollection of his grandfather's preaching probably played no small part in developing the zealous and evangelical tone that appears in his criticism.

From his father, Grigg Matthew Thompson, he would have derived the same kind of influence. Yet for some reason the father scarcely appears in the son's writings, and other records of him are meager. Born in Missouri in 1811, reared in the Whitewater country of Indiana, married at nineteen, he apparently followed his father early into the ministry, remaining for several years after his marriage. in the Whitewater country. Before settling in North Georgia in the 1850's, he had lived in Missouri, again in Indiana, and in Kentucky. There are suggestions, but no conclusive evidence, that he was a man of some prominence in the ministry. His son said that he was "an orator of great power" and though "not an educated man, . . . has written books of a doctrinal sort very popular with his religious denomination."[8]

James Maurice Thompson was born September 9, 1844, in the village of Fairfield, Indiana.[9] Although his published writings as well as unpublished autobiographical notes give the impression that he and his younger brother Will were the only children of the family, one anonymous biographer asserts that Maurice was the fifth child. And in an unpublished account of Sherman's forces overrunning his family home near Calhoun, Georgia, Thompson speaks of "my sisters."[10] Chronology would indicate, or at least allow, a few children before Maurice, because his parents had been married fourteen years when he was born. But whatever the size of the family, it is obvious that Maurice and Will were unusually devoted to each other, to the exclusion of other brothers and sisters.

Of Thompson's early boyhood, before the family settled in Georgia, there is little information. He wrote, "Soon after I was born my parents removed to Missouri and settled in the woods of the southeast part of that state."[11] And he told of his experience as "a very little child, going to a backwoods school in Missouri" where all the pupils chewed liquid amber and the teacher chewed tobacco.[12] From Missouri the family returned to Indiana "and thence went to Kentucky where we dwelt until I was a boy of nine or ten."[13] The location is not specified, though it was probably somewhere in the bluegrass region, the old home of Wilson Thompson. This assumption is strengthened by the fact that Maurice set one of his earliest attempts at fiction, the chief character of which is plainly autobiographical, in Clark County "about six miles south of the little village of Kiddville."[14] Clark County lies just east of Lexington.

At about this time, if not earlier, Thompson's interest in birds began to develop, for he wrote many years later of the boyhood experience of "lying in a dark old wood in Kentucky and watching a pileated woodpecker at work on a dead tulip-bough."[15] There is also brief mention of another school sometime during these wanderings, or possibly another incident at the same school. Thompson was sent by his parents to spend the winter with an uncle, so that he might attend an "old field" school. On the uncle's advice he thrashed the ground with every boy in his class, just to get off on the right foot, only to be thrashed in turn by the teacher.[16]

About 1853 or 1854 the family moved to a farm of two or three hundred acres in the valley of the Coosawattee River of North Georgia, in Gordon County, near the town of Calhoun. Here, for all practical purposes, the son's education began, for it was here that his quick mind and boundless curiosity found unique opportunities to cultivate the interests that distinguish his mature writings: literature and history; hunting, fishing, and bowshooting; bird study and geology. There was, first, the library of poetry, history, and romance collected by his mother. And because the father was an itinerant, the mother's taste had unusual influence with the sons. Second, the red hills on all sides of the plantation supported a profusion of vegetation: pine, oak, and hickory forests, with enough chestnut trees to afford many an outing after the first heavy frost of the fall. The woods were filled with deer, squirrel, rabbit, and turkey, and flocks of songbirds, especially during the migratory periods. The clear, spring-fed rivers meandering through the valleys, now banked by marshes, now by low bluffs, held schools of perch, bream, and bass. These rivers were also the homes of a wide variety of aquatic animals and birds: herons, kingfishers, wood ducks, otters, weasels. The outcroppings of the hills were of sedimentary formation and offered unusual opportunities for the study of paleontology and structural geology. Whether nature and circumstances generated Thompson's interests in all these things or merely nurtured them, it would be fruitless to speculate. But one thing is clear: the Cherokee hills and young Maurice Thompson were peculiarly suited to each other.

The Thompsons moved into the Cherokee country at the end of the white settlement. The Cherokees had been moved out some fifteen years earlier at the insistence of land-hungry, and gold-hungry, white settlers; and by the middle 1850's the picturesque, but not particularly fertile, valleys that had been sporadically cultivated by the Indians were settled by farmers, for, as it turned out, the gold mining was unprofitable—except for a few people like John C. Calhoun who came early and had extensive resources to carry on the work. Farming, too, was unprofitable. Although the climate was mild, the land was not sufficiently rich and flat for extensive cotton plantations in the manner of the central plateau and low country of the state. Some of the hill farmers owned slaves, but they were as much a mark of status as an economic necessity. The principal crops were corn, tobacco, and grain, which were carried to market in wagons or on barges and keel-boats floated down the little rivers—the Salliquoy, the Conasauga, the Oothgaloga, the Coosawattee, the Oostanaula, and the Etowah—that traversed the principal valleys. All these eventually became the Coosa River at the market center of Rome.

On the whole it is doubtful whether anything more than a very moderate prosperity was possible for the hill farmers; the fact that the Thompsons were able to engage an occasional tutor for their sons might be as much an indication that the tutors were inexpensive as that the family was affluent. In a magazine piece Thompson portrayed one of his tutors as an ineffectual and atrabilious young man from Savannah;[17] and if he was representative, they were impoverished young men who had been raised in gentle circumstances but who now found a subordinate post in the household of a preaching hill farmer preferable to economic hardship in Augusta or Savannah. None of them was ever mentioned with affection, or even with respect, by his erstwhile student. There was, however, a hidden advantage to this situation in that the student was allowed to develop his own enthusiasms, as he might not have done under a domineering tutor. For instance, he gave the acquiescent tutor to understand that in Greek it was "poetry, not grammar, that I would have, and nothing else."[18]

It was an irregular and picturesque regimen that the boys lived under. The idyllic nature of the life in North Georgia that was possible before the war Thompson nostalgically expressed in his essay "A Fortnight in a Palace of Reeds." It is April, and through rifts in the forest of pine, hickory, oak, and tulip, grassy glades shine, miniature prairies peculiar to that region. "The young hickory trees spread out marvelous leaves, more than a span in width, and the yellow tulip exaggerates both foliage and flowers. The dogwood and sour gum, the red-oak, the maple and the chestnut, the cherry, the sassafras, and the lovely sweet gum all flourish in the fullest luxury of life and color." Wild flowers cover the valley slopes and fill the ravines. The odors of sassafras and wild plum blossoms mingle and fill the air. In this Arcadia the boys set up their camp in a moss-carpeted area between two wild plum trees, over which a thick-leaved vine has made a connecting canopy and around which, except for a small opening, tall gold-green reeds make a wall. "The earth is warm, the sky is pure and cloudless. Deep in the brake a hermit-thrush is calling. A vireo beyond the river quavers mournfully."[19]

There was little distinction between summer and winter, as far as the boys' studies went. The climate was sufficiently mild to allow outings at any time of the year, and they frequently mixed outdoor life with their studies. As a general rule they tried to spend extra time at their books on Mondays, Tuesday, and Wednesdays in order to have the privilege of spending Thursdays, Fridays, and Saturdays in the woods. But even in the woods their books went along—Alexander Wilson, Audubon, Cicero, Horace, Theocritus—and a schedule of an hour's study alternating with a half hour's bowshooting or fishing was adhered to. When the weather permitted, extended camping trips were the order, their tutor going along and improvising a schoolroom from a shade tree and a mossy log, and the boys conning their books at night by the light of pine-knot flares.[20]

Just how far the woods replaced the conventional schoolroom it would be hard to say. One of Thompson's later biographers made him almost a nineteenth-century version of Beattie's Minstrel, asserting that "he was but twelve years old when he refused to study any longer inside the house and began to take his books to the woods."[21] His later memories of this period were a curious melange of shooting, fishing, reading, woodcraft, boating, sketching, water-coloring, and camp-loafing. Two habits which he acquired during this period are especially important in any consideration of his development as a writer: the habit of sketching, at which he was quick and passably accurate, and that of taking copious notes on the ground at the moment of impression. Another habit of this period, which in later life generated no small number of quasi-literary essays, was that of carrying a pocket edition of some classic —Theocritus and Montaigne were his later favorites—through which he would browse as he rested under a tree or on a river bluff after some vigorous sport with bow or rod. When these episodes became the subjects of autobiographical sketches, they produced an original, if frequently crochety, mixture of art, nature, and criticism.

The genesis of the poetic impulse in Maurice Thompson was also intimately tied up with his life in the woods, or at least it seemed so to him in retrospect. In an essay to which he gave the disillusioned title "A Siren's Whisper" he told of a camping trip with his brother Will and a certain black "Erebus," during which he was smitten with the incurable and disastrous urge toward poetry. The crucial episode occurred one afternoon when Will and Erebus had left him in his hammock: "Now and again I heard Will's long-bow give forth its whizzing shaft, or the arbalest of Erebus recoil with a sullen whack; the tireless two were in the full tide of elemental happiness, glorying in the ancient freedom of savagery. I swung and gazed and listened; the landscape took on a tender countenance, as if to weave over me the maternal spell, and presently there surged up in my soul the sudden consciousness of rhyme and rhythm and color; and a vague voice said to me: 'Be a poet!' Like a quaff of subtle poison, delicious, inevitably deadly, the suggestion left its worry in my blood forever."[22]

Whether this episode is literally true or not, Thompson's telling it reveals his extreme Romantic attitudes toward art and suggests why the urban influence in art, and in life, was anathema to him. Wild nature is the source of the artist's inspiration—discipline and study only stultify. The artist is cursed as well as blessed; he is doomed to suffer, but his bleeding heart is a mark of distinction. When we realize that these attitudes were already old-fashioned by mid-century, we understand one reason why Thompson remained a minor poet and why, in his criticism, he always stood for extreme conservatism.

On Thompson's study and reading during his formative years there is but little specific information. He said, "I had good private teachers now and again, in the mathematics [sic] of which I always have been passionately fond and for which I had such affinity that I never had any trouble in their [sic] study at all—in the Greek, the Hebrew, the Latin, the German and the French languages, so that I get on even now [1887] very well in Latin and know the French well. I studied Kant, Leibnitz and Spinoza—in a way; worshipped Poe for awhile—then idolized Victor Hugo in a boyish abandon; turned back to Roman literature and got the *Somnium Scipionis* by heart, and finally lost myself in the Greek lyrists."[23] Among the Greeks he mentioned specifically Theocritus, and his later devotion to Sappho suggests an early acquaintance. Of the Latin poets, he mentioned, in addition to Cicero, Ovid and Horace; and it is inconceivable that even the most indifferent tutor would have omitted Virgil. His reading in French included Chateaubriand, Fénelon, and Rousseau as well as Victor Hugo.[24] He recalled that his first acquaintance with "The Raven" was made in 1859 from a newspaper in which his lunch was wrapped and that he was completely spellbound.[25] In the same year he first read the works of Lowell; Bryant, Longfellow, Whittier, and Emerson he read "during the last days of slavery."[26] One of his tutors, he recalled, read him *Major Jones's Courtship* when he was a boy, and both Simms and Longstreet he had seen and listened to by the time he was fifteen. He told of hearing Simms discourse on the ills of southern literature, his thesis being that the artist in the South was stifled because he was not allowed to treat the institution of slavery impartially.[27] Thompson later insisted on this same thesis in his criticism of southern literature. Longstreet, as a Methodist minister, visited the Thompson plantation during the 1850's "when there was some keen theological sparring, and heavy slugging, too, between the Methodists and Baptists."[28] The boy's chief impression was disappointment to find that the great man did not resemble the picture of Sir Walter Scott that hung in his room.

That his room should be so decorated is both appropriate and typical: appropriate because in later years, and possibly even then, Scott was the greatest English novelist for him—when Scott was made the mould was broken—and typical because it is a truism of literary history that any antebellum southern family that pretended to culture had to give a prominent place in the library to Scott. Thompson's mother was probably chiefly responsible for his knowledge of Scott and other English writers. In 1887 he wrote, "To her I owe everything. Her intimate knowledge of the best English literature, especially that of Shakespeare, Scott, Byron, Shelley and Keats, was early impressed upon me."[29] Elsewhere he mentioned Tennyson and emphasized that peculiar reverence in which Shakespeare was held. He was required to wash his face, comb his hair, and put on a broad white collar before being allowed to take down the large, heavy-ribbed volume "called by the sacred name of Shakespeare."[30] Even during his war experience he continued to read. While stationed at Thunderbolt, near Savannah, he read the works of Carlyle and DeQuincey. His reading habit extended even to times of action: "While I was a scout, in 1864, I was chided by my superiors for carrying one of Hugh Miller's books around with me."[31]

Important as his reading must have been in developing his literary attitudes, his experiences with nature were also important; in these experiences, archery played a large part. That he is remembered now by archers as the man, who, with his brother Will, revived the sport in America, and that he was identified when his first book of poetry appeared in 1883 as "the archer poet," make his archery activities of even greater interest. The details of just how he first came to the bow are lost, but the implication of one of his early magazine articles on archery is that he and Will first took up the "bow and arrow," as most boys do at some time, as a toy.[32] They must have passed quickly beyond the toy stage, however, because when he was in his middle teens Maurice owned an English bow, which would have been no small investment.[33] But it was not until he and his brother had been practising archery for some years and had gained considerable skill in making their own equipment that the real possibilities of the sport were revealed to them by a certain Thomas Williams, a hermit whose cabin stood in the pine forest that bounded one side of the Thompson farm. Where he learned his archery the boys never discovered, but he was an expert in the classic English style, using the six-foot bow and the cloth-yard shaft. When he began to instruct the boys, they realized to their chagrin that most of what they had learned

on their own would have to be discarded. But they applied themselves with characteristic enthusiasm, and, according to Maurice,
they were "real" archers after "a year or two of training under
Williams and a great deal of hunting among the hills and along
the fine streams of North Georgia."[34]

Learning his archery in the woods, Maurice was always more
interested in hunting than in target shooting; and most of his
hunting was for birds, for ornithology was another lifelong interest
that was nurtured by the Cherokee country. His serious interest
in it might have begun with the commission he received from a
London friend of his father for three woodpecker skins suitable for
mounting.[35] At any rate, while still in his teens, he was observing
birds through a small telescope, sketching them, mounting them,
dissecting them, and avidly reading Wilson and Audubon. Thompson's early interest in geology likewise developed out of a commission, but of a different sort. Out of boyish curiosity he followed
a man who was hunting fossils near the plantation until the
fossil hunter hired him (wage: one trilobite and some quartz crys-
tals) to carry his specimen basket.[36] As he grew older, his interest in
ornithology turned his geological studies toward fossils of birds.

Thus far, the picture that emerges is that of a pair of rather
unusual boys: exclusive, devoted to each other, irregularly but well
educated (Will Thompson later attended Calhoun Academy and
Georgia Military Institute), living a free and half-wild life. But
in other ways their lives were not unusual for the place and time.
They had to work, as did most farm boys,[37] although their farm
labors apparently interfered very little with their nature studies.
They undoubtedly had their share of churchgoing, as the sons of
a minister. They went regularly to town on court days at Calhoun.
the Gordon County seat; their interests there were the same as
those of other boys in the neighborhood—to see the fights and the
horse-swapping and to learn how to swear picturesquely.[38] Moreover, they enjoyed a good deal of social intercourse with their
mountain neighbors. Thompson said that he "grew up a mountaineer boy." He spoke the mountain lingo, wore the mountain
garb, and conformed to all the customs and manners of the mountain folk for many years. "With a flint-lock, 'whole-stock' rifle I
shot in competition at the matches for beef and turkey; I danced
at many a cabin ball where the fiddler played 'Natchez under the
Hill,' 'Black-Eyed Susan,' 'Cotton-Eyed Joe,' and 'Flat Woods,' and

where the loose board floor rattled merrily under our jigging feet. I went to singing-school and to class-meetings, to weddings and to funerals, to still-house meets; I went coon-hunting by torchlight, chesnut-hunting on the mountain tops, 'possum-hunting in the bottom lands, and was always present at the particular justice court ground where a fight was expected. Moreover I chewed 'mounting-twist' tobacco and smoked the same, until I became aware of better habits and reformed."[39] Thompson, like many a "preacher's kid," was not an overly pious young fellow. The Primitive Baptists had strict prohibitions against drinking, gambling, and dancing, and a life such as he described would, if known, have gotten him into serious trouble with his father's congregation. Another evidence of an unregenerate boyhood is a story told by Thompson's mother to her grandchildren. Once when the boys were being punished by their father out behind the woodshed, she hid in the shed, intending to intervene if the strapping became too harsh. As the wails rose in remarkable volume the strapping was cut short, but the wails continued even as the father walked back toward the house; they stopped abruptly when he was out of earshot. Then she heard Maurice say, "See, Willie, what'd I tell ye? They's no fool like an old fool."[40]

The question of Maurice Thompson's experience with slavery necessarily comes up at this point, and it is not an easy one to answer. At first thought, it would seem unlikely that the Thompsons managed a farm of two or three hundred acres without slave labor, and in most of the biographical sketches that have appeared to date there is the inference that Grigg Thompson, as a plantation owner, was a slaveholder. Moreover, Maurice said explicitly that Wilson Thompson was a defender, on the Book, of the institution of slavery.[41] Finally, there is Thompson's service in the Confederate army in defense of, among other things, slavery. But the Cherokee country was not cotton country; corn was the main crop, with some grain and tobacco. Much of that area was still timbered, and it is quite possible, even probable, that only a part of the Thompsons' "two or three hundred" acres was arable. In fact, Thompson's vagueness about the size of the farm suggests that it was wild country, not even easily surveyed. Moreover, the Thompsons were not southerners of the planter class. They came from a border state and belonged to a social group, the Scotch-Irish yeoman farmers, who were nicknamed "the Yankees of the South."[42]

When one looks in Thompson's writings for concrete evidence or statements on the matter, there are none to be found. All this makes the usual inference that the Thompsons owned slaves a doubtful one. Before the war the ratio of non-slaveholders to slaveholders among the independent farmers of the state as a whole was two to one.[43] Add to this the fact that the slave-based economy prevailed in the piedmont area and the coastal plain, not in the hills, and the mathematical probabilities are even more strongly against the Thompsons' owning slaves. However, since he grew up in a slave state and served in the Confederate army, Maurice was thoroughly exposed to all the variant forms of the southern defense of slavery. In later life, though he never defended slavery as an institution, his anti-Negro bias was strong.

The war itself is for a biographer more a dividing line than a period in Thompson's life because so little is known of the part he played in it. In the disorganized mass of autobiographical notes which he sent in 1887 to a prospective biographer, William Malone Baskervill, he made such statements as these: "For reasons which I may divulge to you some time, I cannot give to the world the history of my career in the C. S. Army. I will say this much: I served with a stainless record from '62 to '65 and was honorably surrendered May 1865 at (or near) Kingston Ga. I was an enthusiastic soldier wherever I served. I was noted as a reckless rider and a fine shot." "I was with the 63rd Ga. regiment stationed at Thunderbolt near Savannah." "I was a scout in 1864." "I surrendered with Gen Wofford's command at Kingston, Ga. May 1865." "If you have chanced to read my paper: *Genius and Enthusiasm* in this week's *Independent* [March 17, 1887] you may have noted the account of a young soldier cutting down a telegraph pole under fire. Well, you may say, if you like, that you chance to know that *I* was that *boy!*" "I was and am still passionately attached to the South and I stayed with her until the fight closed, but for the last year of the struggle, the feeling was growing within me that we were battling against the 19th century."[44] In an unpublished manuscript called "The Rape of the Engine" he recounted that he and other bystanders at the Calhoun station joined the pursuit of the Andrews raiders, April 12, 1862. Another unpublished manuscript, "In Sherman's Path," indicates that he took part in the battle of Resaca and a few days thereafter, while visiting his own home, was forced to fall back with a strange Confederate unit as Federal troops overran the plantation. On his way home, he said, he lost contact with the tactical situation because he had carefully avoided meeting Confederate troops from fear that his verbal leave from his commanding officer would not be honored and he would be treated as a deserter.[45] One of Thompson's published poems, "The Ballad of a Little Fun," bears the subtitle "North Georgia Scouts" and tells the story of the death of the unit's leader (whom he calls Jim Polk Edmondson) in a mounted skirmish near the junction of the Coosawattee and Salliquoy rivers. When he sent the poem to Richard Watson Gilder, editor of the *Century*, he said it was based on personal experience that occurred "not far from Resaca."[46] In one of his essays he recalled riding over the battlefield of Chickamauga a week after the battle.[47] In his introduction to *Stories of the Cherokee Hills* he said that "for many months" he served as a scout in North Georgia, North Alabama, and Tennessee.[48] His parole pass dated Kingston, Georgia, May 12, 1865, reads:

> The bearer 3d Lieut. J. M. Thompson of Co. D Johnsons Regiment of Ga Cav. C.S.A. a paroled prisoner of the army of North Ga. has permission to go to his home, and there remain undisturbed.
>
> > By order of
> > Brig Gen'l H. M. Judah
> > s/ Werner W Bjerg
> > Lt Col. Asst Insp Gen'l[49]

His brother Will, writing in 1916, said that Maurice spent over four years in active service, receiving a wound in the right lung from which he suffered a lifelong pulmonary weakness.[50]

These are the data. The problem is to put them into a significant pattern.

Only one of the units mentioned can be identified unmistakably. The 63rd Regiment of Georgia Volunteers was formed in December, 1862, by combining the Oglethorpe Artillery, the Thirteenth Infantry Battalion, and a number of newly recruited separate companies. Its first assignment was to garrison the coast-defense batteries at Thunderbolt and Rosedew Island, near Savannah, under General H. W. Mercer. After General W. T. Sherman began his Atlanta campaign on May 4, 1864, the 63rd became part of a brigade under Mercer ordered to Dalton, Georgia, to reinforce

Joseph E. Johnston's Army of Tennessee, which faced Sherman's forces. This regiment saw hard service throughout the Atlanta campaign; it engaged in the battle of Resaca on May 14 and 15 and distinguished itself at the battle of Kenesaw Mountain from June 19 to June 24. After the evacuation of Atlanta it was a part of General John B. Hood's force during the fall of 1864, when he attempted to divert Sherman by thrusting up into southern Tennessee. In the spring of 1865, decimated by casualties and desertions, it was consolidated with two other depleted units into the First Georgia Regiment and took part in the campaign of the Carolinas under General Johnston.[51]

Since the 63rd Regiment was not formed until December of 1862 and since Thompson mentioned no earlier unit, his military service probably did not begin much before that date. He was not yet in service when he joined in the pursuit of the Andrews raiders in April, 1862. Company I was organized in Gordon County, September, 1862,[52] and it is possible that he was a member. Since he said that he was a scout in 1864, presumably he spent 1863 with the regiment at Thunderbolt. Thompson's statement that he spent "many months" as a scout in North Georgia, North Alabama, and Tennessee would fit with the fact that the 63rd took part in the Atlanta campaign and in Hood's Tennessee campaign. However, he evidently was not with the 1st Georgia Regiment in the Carolina campaign during the spring of 1865.

The other two units with which Thompson was connected—the North Georgia Scouts and Johnson's Regiment of Georgia Cavalry —cannot be identified in either the Confederate or Federal official histories of the war. However, the "Jim Polk Edmondson" named by Thompson as the leader of the North Georgia Scouts can be identified. Federal dispatches list him as Major Thomas Polk Edmonson, leader of a guerilla band, who was killed April 3, 1865, near McLoath Ford, or Hogan's Ford, on the Coosawattee River a few miles above Calhoun. He is first mentioned in a dispatch of October 20, 1864, from the Federal commander at Dalton, Georgia: "There is a man by the name of Edmonson about this country, hanging and killing men and women. He has about seventy-five men with him." On April 1, 1865, a Federal expedition commanded by Lieutenant Colonel Werner W. Bjerg (who signed Thompson's parole pass a month later) set out from Dalton to patrol the area from Dalton to the Coosawattee. By April 3, after repeated skirmishes, they had taken a number of prisoners, killed several of the guerillas including Edmonson, and destroyed the band's distillery.[53] Thompson was apparently a member of this band.

His belonging to a guerilla band would square with his statement that he surrendered with General William T. Wofford's command. Even before Sherman's invasion the mountains of North Georgia had been full of deserters and bands of bushwhackers. After the invasion the situation was almost completely chaotic. Ostensibly the area was occupied by Federal troops, but they could do little more than maintain the railroad line of communication from Chattanooga to Atlanta, because the rest of the country was in the hands of irregulars, some with Union and some with southern sympathies—and some with neither. "Throughout north Georgia thieving and murdering were widespread. Thousands of deserters were prowling through the country, robbing for their living. Many of them were mounted and passed as scouts, claiming to be Texans."[54] The depredations became so numerous that on January 23, 1865, the Confederate War Department directed General Wofford to assume command of Confederate forces in North Georgia and instructed him "to break up unauthorized military organizations, arrest deserters, and restore civil and military law. He secured seven thousand men, many of whom were deserters."[55] Through his efforts, order of a sort was restored, and with the cooperation of the Federal commander, General Judah, he distributed supplies to relieve the distress of the civilian population. The North Georgia Scouts was evidently one of the "unauthorized organizations" that Wofford broke up, after the death of its leader, and Thompson, when brought under official control again, was evidently assigned to a provisional unit called Johnson's Cavalry. Perhaps such irregular service is what Thompson had in mind when he hinted to Baskervill of mysteries in his war record; however, this assumption would not explain what he meant when he said that he served with "stainless record." Something more is needed.

His brother's statement is the only evidence that he was wounded, though there is much evidence of a pulmonary weakness. Some ten years after the war he wrote, "When I was in the army, I was actually discharged for lung *tuberculosis*. I had hemorrages [*sic*]. The doctors begged me to die, but I took a notion to do no such thing. I *went back* to the army at the end of 60 days and served to the close of the war."[56] In later life he avoided the rigorous winters of Indiana by taking his family to the Mississippi or Florida Gulf coast, and he died of pneumonia which developed after an attack of grippe. Whatever the precise cause of his pulmonary weakness, his military service was probably responsible for it.

His statement that he was discharged because of tuberculosis also may explain how he ended his service with the 63rd Regiment. If so, his later connection with an irregular unit would not have been the result of desertion but of reenlistment, so to speak. It is even likely that only an irregular unit would accept him for service after he had been medically discharged. These conditions would come much nearer to explaining his statement that his was a "stainless" record.

His two and one-half years of military service, coming in the extremely impressionable period when Thompson was developing into manhood (he was under twenty-one when the war ended), might be expected to have a significant effect on his personality, an effect whose real importance would become increasingly clear as he grew older. This was the case. By temperament more active than contemplative, through romanticizing his war experiences he found it easy to apologize for the active and violent tendencies in American domestic and foreign affairs toward the end of the century. Some of this apology was explicit, in patriotic poetry supporting the Spanish-American War or in essays defending white supremacy and lynch law. Most of it was implicit in his use of violence in his fiction: Alice of Vincennes is one of the most violent, and most patriotic, young ladies in American literature.

After the war, the Thompsons, like most southern families, were in straitened circumstances: their farm was in ruins. According to Thompson's later testimony, the library had been burned and "there was not much left of [the house] when the army was done with it."[57] When the boys were mustered out (Will Thompson had enlisted in the 4th Georgia Infantry in 1863), they came home to a dismal prospect which was fulfilled during the next few years. North Georgia had its share of carpetbaggers; there were political troubles with them and with their Negro supporters, and there were even some lynchings. In one of these affairs Thompson learned a dear lesson when he tried to aid the sheriff in talking a mob out of its victim; he was outfoxed by a group who pretended to be convinced of their error and who volunteered to escort the prisoner back to jail while he and the sheriff harangued the uncertain mob. This taught him that lynch mobs are not always hysterical rabble but are often motivated by a calm and purposeful core of influential men.[58]

Day-to-day life in Calhoun was by no means so exciting. There was no prospect in planting, but the outlook for the professions was a little better. So for the first summer Thompson and his brother worked as field hands during the day and pursued their studies in mathematics, engineering, and law at night.

Literature claimed some of his attention, too. Although Oliver Wendell Holmes is the only author mentioned specifically as being studied at this time, there almost certainly were many others, for this was his first period of serious literary activity. He attempted criticism, fiction, verse, and philosophical essays—sometimes mixing the genres into a curious potpourri. At any rate these early attempts reflect a study of Longfellow, Poe, Ticknor, Tennyson, Virgil, Spinoza, Leibnitz, and Kant. His outlet at this time was *Scott's Monthly Magazine* of Atlanta, according to Frank Luther Mott the most important of the more than twenty ephemeral southern magazines of literary intent that existed for brief periods between 1865 and 1870. Its chief claim to fame was that it published the early work of Sidney Lanier and Paul Hamilton Hayne.[59] An Atlanta newspaper hack, James W. Davidson, wrote in 1869, in a sketch full of factual errors, that Thompson was "known for a number of years as a contributor to most of the literary periodicals South and some North."[60] But whatever the accuracy of Davidson's statement, the fact of Thompson's inclusion in the book indicates that he was beginning to make a literary name for himself before he left Georgia.

The disadvantages under which he worked are suggested in his letters to Baskervill. He wrote of shooting and selling squirrels at ten cents each for enough money to buy a Greek lexicon and some engineering works. He sold cider made in a homemade press to buy other books. Even candles were a luxury, and study was done in front of an open fireplace by the flaring light of pine knots gathered in the woods. In later life he had a special regard for the books he had bought so dearly and conned so carefully during these years.[61]

In addition to the money, hunting also afforded an excuse to revisit some of the picturesque and isolated mountain pockets which he had not seen for nearly ten years. This gave him the opportunity to absorb through a more mature sensibility the racy details that later went into his dialect stories and sketches of the area. It was during this same period that he had a brief but not very successful law practice with his father in Calhoun.[62]

The other important experiences in the years immediately after the war were his explorations and scientific studies in Florida and southeastern Georgia. In one sense they were only extended hunting trips, perhaps undertaken with the hope of making a little money in the expanding market for heron-plumes. They also had a thera-peutic purpose—to strengthen Thompson's weak lungs. But they were much more to him. They offered, of course, opportunities for further scientific studies—on one of them he made the first serious attempt of record to catalog the flora and fauna of the Okeechobee region. More important, they were an indulgence of his almost mystic affinity for the near-savage life. As he wrote to Baskervill, "I was impelled to go into the wilds of Nature and went." Though he may have been unaware of it, these experiences in the wilder-ness supplied him with the kind of literary material that was peculiarly in demand at the time and also injected a strong element of primitivism into his developing attitudes toward art and society.

The chronology of the various trips is hazy. Thompson said in one of his early archery articles that he and his brother spent three winters in Florida "shooting over some of the finest water and land region for sporting to be found in the world."[63] The winter of 1867-68 he spent exploring Lake Okeechobee, the upper St. John's River and the Kissimmee River with the aid of three "crackers" who had spent the war years on the lake to escape military service.[64] The exploration of Okefenokee swamp was prob-ably not so extensive. Will Thompson related that they went there in July, 1866, and that Maurice was at this time still convalescing from his lung wound.[65] This would leave the winters of 1865 and 1866 unaccounted for specifically, but apparently one of them was spent on the St. John's River and the other among the marshes, islands, and inlets of the Indian River, the name given to the nar-row sound formed by the barrier islands along the middle of Florida's east coast. On both these trips they were accompanied by a Negro man of all work, Caesar, who, along with the boat and part of their equipment, was furnished by a certain Leonidas Berkeley, a trader with headquarters somewhere on Indian River. Of personal associations during this period very little is recorded.

On one occasion a British hunting party visited the camp which the brothers had established on Indian River; it is implied that the Britishers were archers also. The brothers also made the acquaintance of a family of hermits (if that is not a contradiction in terms), whose life, close to nature, profoundly impressed Maurice as did his contact with an Indian, known only as Tommy, who had left his tribe and elected to live a solitary life in the wilderness because of his disdain for the firearms which his tribesmen were coming to prefer to the ancient bow and arrow. It is not certain whether he met Tommy during the 1860's or on a later trip to Florida after he was established in Indiana; but it was some time before 1875 when he wrote of the experience.[66]

During the spring of 1868 the brothers, seeing that most of the opportunities in the South were for northerners, decided to reverse the procedure of the carpetbaggers and try their luck in the North. The Reconstuction Acts of a hostile Congress, beginning in 1867, and Andrew Johnson's impeachment in February of 1868 no doubt were factors in their decision, as well as the knowledge that Thompsons had once prospered in Indiana. Whatever the ultimate reasons, they made bundles of what possessions they could carry and started north afoot, arriving in Indiana "absolutely penniless."[67]

Crawfordsville lies about forty-five miles west of Indianapolis in rolling, fertile country. Founded about 1823, it had profited by the establishment there of a government land office, and in the spring of 1868 it was a prosperous town of about three thousand: a banking and marketing center for a very rich farming area then being developed out of the swamps that had earlier made the area, in Thompson's phrase, "an ague-plagued wilderness." It was also the seat of Wabash College, which was founded in 1832 and by 1868 was a highly regarded institution in the Midwest. The town was dominated by the Elstons, the family of the leading banker. Banker Elston had a bevy of forceful and talented daughters, one of whom had married Henry S. Lane, who later became governor, senator, and first national chairman of the Republican party. Another daughter, Susan, had married General Lew Wallace, an alumnus of Wabash College, who had lived in Crawfordsville since 1853. In addition to Wallace, three other recently retired Union generals lived there. It was a strongly pro-Union and a strongly Republican town. Economically it was advancing rapidly; the

Monon Railroad had been serving the town for some years and the Indianapolis, Bloomington, and Western and the Vandalia railroads were soon to be completed.

Perhaps it was the railroad-building that attracted the two slender, sinewy young men from the South. At any rate they made their way to Crawfordsville, and Maurice Thompson found employment as a civil engineer with John Lee, a member of a pioneer Crawfordsville family and at that time a section contractor on the I.B.&W. (now the Peoria and Eastern division of the New York Central). Thompson was evidently an excellent engineer because he is reputed to have risen within three months to the position of chief engineer. The chances are that he was retained by Lee the next year when, as president of the Logansport division of the Terre Haute and Indianapolis Railroad (part of the Vandalia), Lee began its construction. Begun in the fall of 1869, it was completed in about two years. According to another statement, Thompson was chief engineer of the L.C.&S.W. Railroad "and ran the first line of that road from Frankfort to Kokomo, and thence to Lima, Ohio."[68] At any rate we have Thompson's testimony that he began at a salary of $75 a month and within three months was making $300 a month, a very substantial figure in 1868.[69]

It was while working for John Lee that he met his wife Alice, the railroad-builder's eldest daughter. Marriage followed quickly, probably in August or September of 1868. He wrote to the editor of *Scott's* in time for the note to be published in the September issue, "I have just been married to Miss Alice R. Lee, a beautiful and accomplished girl of seventeen."[70]

John Lee's section of the Vandalia was completed in 1871. In the same year Thompson began the practice of law. For the first three years after their marriage he and his young wife had been living wherever his work took them. Now they settled in Crawfordsville;[71] and Thompson began to realize to the fullest what it was to be a southerner in a northern Republican town. In the autobiographical *A Banker of Bankersville* he reflected on that experience. In spite of the fact that the young southerner portrayed there had labored to cast off all the peculiarities of southern character which he felt might hinder his adaptation to the new life, he was the frequent butt of malicious wit, of which the following quip from the editor of the *Snarler* is typical: "Our solitary relic of 'Chivalry and honahsah' will wave the ensanguined garment over the jury next week."[72] But Thompson, like young Milford of his novel, stuck with the law until he felt that he had gone to the head of the local bar, which, incidentally, was a strong one in that part of the state.[73]

It was during this period that his friendship with Lew Wallace began, a friendship which prospered in spite of the seventeen-year difference in their ages and the fact that they had been on opposite sides during the war. Wallace recalled that his first sight of the impressive young man was in court, but their friendship developed on the basis of their common interests in sports and literature more than in law. They hunted and fished together on Sugar Creek and in the Kankakee swamps; they exchanged manuscripts and spent long hours discussing literature. Thompson's enthusiasm for *The Fair God* played a large part in Wallace's decision to offer this first novel to a publisher.[74]

Will Thompson married Alice's sister Ida in 1874, and in succeeding years the brothers and their wives took an increasingly active part in the social life of the town. In May, 1874, they organized an archery club, the Wabash Merry Bowmen, and were the guiding spirits on many an outing when both ladies and gentlemen tried their skill at sylvan targets and after a picnic supper rode back to town by moonlight. In the fall of 1877, there was an excursion to northern Michigan, which seems to have been made by a large party from Crawfordsville.[75] Such social activities indicate at least a moderate financial success for the brothers' law partnership. In 1881 Thompson estimated that he would make about a thousand dollars in "three or four months." He offered this as an argument against his striking out on a purely literary career.[76] He said that his wants were legion; his taste for books and social life and his growing family militated against relying on the uncertain literary market for his livelihood.

Thompson's home for several years after he settled in Crawfordsville was a small cottage crowded with books and mementos of his literary friendships;[77] it was here that the Thompson children were born—two boys and two girls. The eldest, John Grigg, died January 15, 1876, at the age of five. The other son, Claude, and the two daughters, Jessie and Agnes, all survived their father.

Although Thompson was "driving a big law practice" during the 1870's, he again went into the railroad business with his father-in-law. In 1875 and 1876 he was chief engineer of the

Indianapolis and Springfield Railroad, of which Lee was president. In November, 1875, Thompson wrote that he was "under full headway building" near Rockville, Indiana, and that he was both engineer and lawyer for the railroad.[78]

Law and railroading served Thompson as a springboard into politics. In 1876 he campaigned all over the state for the Democratic party,[79] and in 1878 he was a successful candidate for the legislature. His election indicates that he was an impressive candidate, for he ran as a Democrat in a strongly Republican area. Of course there may have been other factors, such as a split within the Republican ranks, but in his own mind at least he was a successful politician. He once asserted that at a time when he saw his way clear to go to Congress and beyond, he had given up politics for literature.[80] As will appear, he did not entirely give up politics, but he did give up the idea of making a career of it.

Both as an engineer and as a lawyer, Thompson had been following literature as an avocation. The urge to write was always with him: "The *cacoethes scribendi* was gnawing at me."[81] The result was a steady output during the 1870's. He sold a dime novel, *The League of the Guadalupe,* to Street and Smith at the beginning of the decade.[82] In 1871 he began to contribute local-color sketches, sometimes anonymously, to newspapers, among them the New York *Tribune.*[83] Although he felt that his literary career really began with the publication of "At the Window" in the April, 1873, *Atlantic,* many of his works were in print before that. Considering only such national magazines as *Appleton's, Atlantic, Harper's, Independent, Lippincott's,* and *Scribner's,* his publications during the decade totaled thirty-eight poems and twenty prose pieces, most of which were essays. Add to this some fourteen poems, seven reviews, and six essays in Crawfordsville and Indianapolis papers, and it is clear that the *cacoethes scribendi* was indeed gnawing at him.[84] By 1875 his local-color sketches had been collected in a volume called *Hoosier Mosaics;* and in 1878, because of remarkable reader response, some of his essays on archery from *Scribner's, Harper's,* and *Appleton's* were collected as *The Witchery of Archery.*

As if this productivity were not enough, in 1876 and 1877 he was writing a novel called *At a Hoosier Watering Place,* attempting to get afloat a western literary magazine to be published in Cincinnati, trying to get a volume of poetry published by James R. Osgood,[85] and corresponding with as many literary figures as he could scrape an acquaintance with. Most important of these were Howells, whose friendship grew after he had published Thompson's first poem in the *Atlantic,* and Hayne, a fellow-contributor to *Scott's* whose poetry the younger man reviewed enthusiastically at every opportunity. He also mentioned corresponding with Edgar Fawcett, though none of these letters have been found.

Thompson doubtless would have cast the die for a literary career much sooner than he did had it not been for financial necessity. It was a constant theme in his letters to Hayne. In July, 1874, he asked Hayne directly how much he received for his poems. In February, 1876, he said,

> I am doing literally nothing now in the way of writing. I am too full of business. I am a little in debt, but am paying off rapidly. One year will, if I keep my health, leave me free to take up my pen with a little competency to sustain me. I have a charming little home which I have wrung out of nothing in the last three years or so. I have it nearly paid for and furnished to my liking and one more thousand will put me clear of debt. To do this I've pegged my brain almost out. Night and day I've worked regardless of weariness, excitement, loss of sleep, everything. Next fall, if I keep my health and have no other bad mishap, I shall say I owe no man and can let up a little.[86]

In July, 1877, he was still hoping: "I am trying to get a little competency in order to have leisure for art-work and meantime am trying to practice art. This strains me to my best nerve. Truly a competency comes slowly!"

The competency never came; but about 1880 Thompson resolved on a literary career while maintaining a law practice to piece out his income. By 1884 he had given up the practice of law entirely.[87] The most important factors in this final decision were three. The first was a growing disillusionment with the law. As Thompson remembered it in the South, a lawyer had been a respected professional man who was expected to conduct himself like a gentleman, but in the boisterous and bustling Midwest he was as often as not expected to be a hustler and a brawler. As he said of his young lawyer in *A Banker of Bankersville,* "He nursed high notions of the dignity of the profession; as if he had lived in the golden age of the law, when to be a lawyer was a very high honor."[88] And he no doubt experienced, like young Milford, the prick of conscience at the realization that these blunt Hoosier farmers regarded him just as they did a field hand. He was expected, for his retainer, to work their will on their enemies, as the field hand was expected, for his wages, to work their will on a meadow that needed ditching or a pasture that needed mowing. Constantly in his mind was the vision of a sedate and satisfying life which the Indiana bar could not afford: he wrote to Howells, "I envy you now in your quiet room weaving the cloth of gold, whilst I am hammering and quarreling in the graceless court room."[89]

This friendship with Howells was the second important factor, for in addition to encouragement about his work, he received a visit from Howells in the spring of 1881. Howells was in search of the details of a western divorce trial for use in *A Modern Instance.* As a lawyer Thompson was in a position to oblige him; consequently, Howells spent a few days in May as Thompson's guest, while he observed, with Thompson's explanations, a divorce proceeding in the Montgomery County Court. Thompson wrote of the visit, "Your recent stay with us . . . was a memorable and is a cherished event in our quiet home life."[90]

Earlier in the year, Thompson had made a trip to Florida to sketch scenes and to gather material for *A Tallahassee Girl.*[91] Now Howells, upon returning to Boston, undertook to get his own publisher, Osgood, to buy the novel on the strength of Thompson's material and plan and thus give Thompson the opportunity to "make one trial with undivided strength."[92] Osgood would not commit himself without seeing the finished product, but he was willing to offer a 10 per cent royalty, with a guarantee of $500, if he liked it. This still meant that Thompson would have to take three months out of his law practice with no certainty of a return. Only at the urging of his brother Will did he take the chance. Fortunately the project turned out well:[93] Osgood accepted the book in September and published it the following March. On the strength of good reviews and strong sales, Osgood accepted Thompson's next novel, *His Second Campaign,* and published it in June, 1883. Both novels appeared anonymously in the "Round Robin Series," though it was more or less an open secret that Thompson was the author. Soon afterward Osgood published Thompson's first volume of poems, *Songs of Fair Weather,* which was greeted by Howells with a glowing review in the *Independent.*[94] With this notice by a major critic in a major eastern magazine, Thompson must have felt that his career had finally begun.

The third factor in his decision to give up law for writing was the removal of Will to Seattle. The brothers had shared their hunting, their writing, their study, their social life, and their work. When Will, perhaps moved by the knowledge that his brother's real desire was not for a law practice but for a literary career, left late in 1881 or early in 1882,[95] Thompson no longer had a sympathetic partner who could keep the firm going while he pursued his literary work. A visit in November, 1881, to Paul Hamilton Hayne's home, Copse Hill, near Augusta may have delayed his decision, for there he found the man then generally acknowledged as the South's greatest poet living in genteel poverty. At any rate in 1884 he finally abandoned his law practice and set out to earn his living by writing and lecturing.

When Thompson turned to weaving his own cloth of gold, he undertook a regimen which never varied for the rest of his life. Up early in the morning, he went to his desk for an hour or two before breakfast and returned to work until lunch. Afternoons were given to recreation: archery on the lawn, tramps in the woods, a spin out in the country on one of the gravel roads radiating in several directions from Crawfordsville, or fishing in nearby Sugar Creek. Winters were spent somewhere in the South, usually at Bay St. Louis, Mississippi, under the same regimen. To put it his way, he did not believe in vacations; he worked every day and played every day wherever he was.[96] Alice Thompson helped him to maintain this schedule. She was, according to one frequent visitor, an ideal wife for a man of Thompson's temperament: gentle, gracious, comforting, and capable of keeping a well-ordered and tranquil house.[97] Moreover, she shared to a considerable degree his literary interests and his enthusiasm for sports. He dedicated his last book of nature essays to her because, as he said, "she shared the experiences herein recorded, and her influence is in every page. . . . We tramped together in all the places I have described; we camped together on lonely spots; we sat together on the breezy bluffs and read, sketched and made notes. She carried my extra arrows on many a shooting-ground, where the birds were wary and wild."[98]

The state of Thompson's health possibly had something to do with his preference for southern winters. In addition to the pulmonary weakness, by the mid-1880's he appears to have been a chronic sufferer from malaria and rheumatism. He also enjoyed the proximity of Bay St. Louis to New Orleans, where he went often for the theater and opera, for lectures, or just to browse around the French Quarter, particularly in the bookstalls on Royal Street.[99] The antique desk at which he worked for many years he bought there. Always a lover of the picturesque, he was fascinated by the Crescent City.

Thompson's venture into the literary world turned out moderately well during the 1880's, if we may judge by his publication record. In magazines of national reputation and circulation such as the *Atlantic* or the *Independent,* his contributions from 1884 through 1889 totaled seventy-four essays, nineteen poems, and two short stories. When these are considered in addition to his numerous contributions to local and regional journals, we have the foundation for a substantial literary reputation. During this period he published a total of sixty-two essays, ten poems, and six stories in such Chicago magazines as *Current* and *America* and in such newspapers as the Chicago *Times,* the Chicago *Inter-Ocean,* the Indianapolis *Herald,* the Indianapolis *Journal,* the Indianapolis *News,* and the Crawfordsville *Journal.*

He was steadily publishing books, too. Although Osgood had published Thompson's two novels and his volume of poems in 1882 and 1883, his interest in Thompson had apparently waned, for even before Osgood's failure early in 1885, Thompson was making other arrangements. One of his novels, his maiden effort, first called *At a Hoosier Watering Place* and later, *Summer Sweethearts,* he sold to *Outing* magazine for serial publication in 1884. Between 1884 and 1888 he finished and published three other novels. *At Love's Extremes* appeared in June, 1885, under the imprint of Cassell and Company, an English firm recently reorganized and then trying to break into the American market. His next novel, and easily his best, *A Banker of Bankersville,* he offered to Richard Watson Gilder for *Century* magazine. Failing there, he turned again to Cassell and Company, who brought it out late in November, 1886. The third novel was *A Fortnight of Folly,* which appeared in July, 1888, published by the small New York firm of John B. Alden. This firm had already published *By-Ways and Bird Notes* (1885) and *Sylvan Secrets* (1887), both collections of nature essays which had appeared earlier in magazines. A third volume of essays and sketches was *The Boy's Book of Sports* (Century Company, 1886), again a collection of magazine pieces. The other production of the period was a school history in D. Lothrop Company's "Story of the States Series" called *The Story of Louisiana* (1888). By 1889, then, though Thompson had not achieved a firm relationship with a first-rate publisher, he was able to get most of what he wrote in print.

Indicative of his growing reputation were the notices given to his public addresses. He spoke at Wabash College in June, 1885, at Purdue University, June, 1886, and addressed literary groups in Indianapolis from time to time. His relationship with one of these groups—the Western Association of Writers—is a good index to his popularity in the Midwest. From the time of its organization in June, 1886, until its fourth convention in June, 1888, he served as president, although he had no part in the plans which brought the organization into being.[100] Some of his speeches before this organization received national notice, largely because he had the courage to talk plainly to a group which was constantly in danger of becoming a mutual consolation society for unsuccessful authors. The *Critic* hailed him when he said bluntly, "If your literature does not attract attention it isn't worth attention; if you resent this truth you shut out forever your only hope of success."[101]

His warmest acclaim probably came from two speaking engagements at Vanderbilt University in December, 1886, and April, 1888. He had been recommended by Professor Charles Forster Smith to begin a series of lectures by contemporary makers of literature. "He proved to be a good lecturer—simple, natural, totally unaffected, interesting; his voice not powerful, rather gentle and soft, but clear and carrying far. The people flocked to hear him, and speaker and people were mutually pleased."[102] At his second appearance, fifteen months later, his reception was even warmer: "The most beautiful and enthusiastic audience that ever greeted a man."[103]

Thompson was also esteemed as a critic. In 1887 Moses Coit Tyler sent him a complimentary copy of his *History of American Literature, 1607-1765,* indicating Thompson's standing with a very respectable academician.[104] In November, 1888, Richard Watson Gilder asked Thompson to write the sketch of his (Gilder's) life and writings to appear in Moulton's *Library of Literary Criticism,* then in preparation.[105] Two months later he was invited, along with such luminaries as Whittier, Tennyson, E. C. Stedman, Theodore Roosevelt, Andrew Lang, and a host of lesser lights, to contribute to the James Russell Lowell birthday issue of the *Critic*.[106] The *Independent,* commenting on this issue, called the group of writers "the most distinguished we remember to have seen in a single number of any magazine or paper."[107]

In fact, 1889 was a portentous year for Thompson. It marked his "arrival," in a literary sense. On July 4 the ultra-nationalist Chicago weekly *America* announced him as a staff contributor to the literature department. "Hereafter Mr. Maurice Thompson will furnish the leading article to this department each week, *vice* Mr. Julian Hawthorne. . . . The object of the change is to make this department reflect more nearly Western views upon current literary topics. Mr. Thompson, who is a resident of Indiana, of broad and liberal sympathies, thoroughly imbued with the pride and hope of American citizenship, needs no introduction to these columns."[108] Soon after this recognition as an influential man of letters in the Midwest came Thompson's appointment as literary editor of the *Independent,* announced in an editorial of October 3. He had been well known, the editors noted, since 1885 when he "began the critical, ethical articles on fiction and poetry that have brought him most prominently before the American public. These articles have been written with high moral purpose and enthusiasm, and have compelled attention. . . . It is not too much to say that he has an influence second to no man in the country in determining, if not what shall be written, at least what shall be read."[109] His duties as literary editor he shared with Kinsley Twining, D. D., Thompson being charged generally with reviewing novels, poetry, and other belles lettres, while Twining reviewed history, philosophy, and theology.[110] *America* survived only two years after Thompson's association began, but he remained with the *Independent* until his death, when Paul Elmer More took over his duties. Here he enjoyed a unique working arrangement: he never entered the editorial office; everything was sent to him wherever he happened to be.

But these crucial six years between 1884 and 1890 were not without problems. Money, of course, was the main one. In 1885, to supplement his literary income, his political friends obtained for him the office of State Geologist and Chief of the Bureau of Natural History. After the election of a Republican governor in 1888, he had to choose between sacrificing his financial security and resorting to what he regarded as an underhanded trick to keep his office. "I am approaching what must be a chief crisis in my life. . . . I am asked by party friends to go before the incoming Democratic State Legislature and ask them to take the control of my office . . . out of the Rep. Governor's hands so that I can hold it by legislative appointment four more years. . . . I shall not do it. I consider it unworthy of me, poor though I be. I obtained the office honorably and have done my best to make it honorable, and I must leave it by the door I entered. Just what I can do for the future is a question. I must look about."[111] Early the next year he lost the office and was again without a steady source of income.

The impending loss of office may have motivated him to enter a newspaper syndicate scheme with E. E. Hale, Joaquin Miller, Franklin File, and Lew Wallace. Each writer was to furnish a novelette, the whole series to be sold to a group of newspapers, with the profits to be shared equally.[112] The scheme was carried out (Thompson's contribution was *The Lily of Rochon*), but there is no record of the financial returns.

There is little specific information about what Thompson was paid for his writing. He always thought it was not enough. He wrote in one letter that "on the whole" his books paid well, but his other correspondence fails to bear this out. When Gilder paid him $75 for a short story in the *Century,* it drew from him a protest heavy with discouragement and, it must be admitted, a little choleric.[113] In substance, he said that it took a month to write a story and at $75 each he could not afford the time. Four months earlier he had asked Gilder for the name of a good literary agent in New York who would, for a percentage, fight his financial battles for him. "I have been trusting wholly to the editors," he said, "to set the value on my M.S. and they are not all as generous as you."[114] If this "generous" editor paid him $75 for a story published in one of the best magazines in the country, the returns from less generous editors must have provided something less than a living. This is borne out by another letter of the same period in which he said, "I have felt that there ought to be a reasonable and certain income small to be sure, but sufficient for the needs of our unassuming and inexpensive country-town family. . . . This income has not materialized."[115]

The financial problem was symptomatic of a situation which Thompson was sure existed but which no eastern editor would admit. He was an "outsider," and he believed this was because of the fact that he was a westerner and would not kowtow to the New York taste. Time after time he saw what seemed to him preferential treatment given to eastern authors by the major magazines, while his own work was rejected or published only by second-rate outlets. His best novel, *A Bank of Bankersville,* was refused by the *Century,* and though at the time Thompson took the news with equanimity, when shortly afterwards he saw Frank Stockton's flimsy and fantastic *Mrs. Lecks and Mrs. Aleshine* serialized, he entered into a very frank correspondence with Gilder about the matter. "Now you can't blame me for looking surprised when I see nonsense crowd out what I feel is, though not great work, very faithful, earnest and worthy work."[116] He would not be convinced by Gilder's justification of his editorial policy and summed up his case thus: "Now the 'bottom thought' . . . of this matter is: either I have mistaken my calling and am unworthy to be trusted as a writer, or I am an 'outsider,' who is used as a jar of superfluous milk to be skimmed when there chances to be a sudden call for 'copy' or something of the sort—*coquin de bon sort!* Either horn of the dilemma is good for one's liver!"[117]

Thompson's refusal to accept the first horn was not entirely a matter of vanity, for he did have a substantial following in his own region, and for a while this growing local and southern popularity even led him into the trap of regarding himself as an "insider"—on the same plane as Howells and James.

After Thompson's first successful lecture at Vanderbilt University, his friend Baskervill, who was a professor of English at that institution, proposed that they attempt to have a biographical sketch of Thompson included in *Harper's* or *Century.* Thompson eagerly acquiesced and sent him a mass of biographical data and a photograph. *Century* regularly ran such sketches of leading literary figures, and when Gilder declined Baskervill's offering, Thompson realized the truth. Moreover, the news came at a time that made it especially bitter. On his return to Vanderbilt in the spring of 1888 for a reading of his poems, he had received a memorable ovation. Leaving the hall on a crest of popular acclaim and self-confidence, he learned the bad news from Baskervill. He returned to the Maxwell House and took a copy of the new *Century* with him to his room. When he opened it he found an article on Robert Louis Stevenson of precisely the sort that Gilder had refused about him. In a burst of emotion he sat down and wrote, "Oh, Gilder! You know how bitter this is. I am in the dust before the picture of Stevenson in the Current Century and I feel that there could be no more perfect revalation [*sic*] of my insignificance than that which at this moment burns in my very soul. . . . It is the deepest misery I ever felt. If I have an enemy let him gloat."[118] Gilder answered this letter as kindly as he could, and Thompson went on in his reply to explain his feelings more fully: "I am outside the circle, of course, and am kept from exerting a personal influence, and I shall never, perhaps, be inside. The loss to me, just now, is peculiarly great. Simply stated my situation is that of a man who knows that his work is widely prized and appreciated . . . but who cannot just touch good wages for that work. I knew the power of the *Century*. . . . My meridian is at hand. . . . Just now I feel the need of what Mr. Howells had at about my age, the way made clear."[119]

Eighteen months later his association with the *Independent* cleared his way as much as it was ever to be cleared and brought him as near to being an "insider" as he was ever to be.

Although its literary department was important, the *Independent* was not primarily a literary magazine; it was not in the same class as the *Atlantic* or the *Century* or *Harper's*. The differences lay partly in editorial tone, partly in the subscription list. Begun as a Congregational organ, by the 1890's it was a non-sectarian "liberal" religious weekly and boasted the largest number of clergymen among its subscribers of any magazine in the country. Its treatment of all matters, political, literary, or whatever, was marked by a "pronouncedly ethical spirit."[120] Because of this spirit and because of its highly vocal Republicanism, the journal appealed to the solid, conservative middle class, the heirs of that Genteel Tradition which was to reach its final bloom between 1890 and 1914. It was also free of the New England bias that was steadily making the *Atlantic* a less vital influence in the land. Consequently, although the *Independent* did not offer Thompson a niche on the same literary elevation as the *Century* or *Harper's,* it did offer him a highly respectable entree into American middle-class homes all over the country.

Thompson apparently found this niche congenial, for the last decade of his life was an almost incredibly productive period. Between 1890 and his death he published two volumes of poetry, four novels, one volume of short stories, two volumes of essays, and one volume of history. At his death he left in manuscript two volumes of nature essays and a novel, the latter being published within a few months.[121] In national periodicals he published 24 short stories, 45 poems, and 268 essays; in local and regional journals, 6 stories, 19 poems, and 106 essays. This tabulation does not include the unsigned book reviews, averaging two or three per week, which he wrote for the *Independent*. Of course most of his signed work appeared in the *Independent* (172 essays, 33 poems, 1 story), with the Chicago *America* ranking next (55 essays). Also, after December, 1898, he seems to have had some sort of regular connection with the *Saturday Evening Post,* in which he published 55 essays between that time and his death.

He had the same capacity for tremendous literary output that had helped to make Howells a leading figure in the 1880's. This remarkable and steady production, with its consequent repeated impact upon the public mind, made Thompson an important critic during the 1890's. The best indication of his position beyond the already cited statement by the editor of the *Independent,* comes from Edmund Clarence Stedman, the dean of the genteel literati. In 1892 he wrote, "You are about as wholesome, broadminded, independent and well-equipped a critical writer as we have. I read your frequent and impartial sketches always, and consequently find myself in sympathy with your frank views." A few months later he congratulated Thompson on having been attacked in the British press. It is characteristic of the British, he said, that they never notice an American writer until he "knocks them straight between the eyes." Then they sneer and strike below the belt, but they respect one thereafter. That Andrew Lang and John Nichol had attacked Thompson was evidence for Stedman that "what you say henceforth will not be ignored abroad."[122]

Indirect evidence of Thompson's importance is the number of lectureships and honors which he enjoyed during the 1890's. In June, 1891, he was a featured speaker, along with Thomas Nelson Page, at a Chautauqua conclave at Glen Echo, Washington, D.C.[123] In May, 1893, he delivered the Carew Lectures at Hartford Theological Seminary and saw them published the following November as *The Ethics of Literary Art.* In June, 1893, he was invited to read his poem "Lincoln's Grave" before the Harvard chapter of Phi Beta Kappa and was made an honorary member. On July 4 of that year he received a standing ovation at the Roseland Park festival, Woodstock, Connecticut, when he read his patriotic poem "The Bloom o' the World."[124] In June, 1898, he delivered commencement addresses at Emory University and the Pennsylvania College for Women, at Pittsburgh; his letter to President Warren A. Candler of Emory suggests that he was giving several other addresses on the same trip.[125] Boston University invited him to give the commencement address on June 6, 1900, where his reception was such that he was invited to repeat it before the Wabash College chapter of Phi Beta Kappa on June 9.[126] Perhaps on this same occasion, but definitely in 1900, the college conferred upon him the honorary degree of Doctor of Letters. An honor which did not quite materialize was the post of Minister to Mexico. The Buffalo *Times* of February 20, 1895, carried the following wry comment: "Powerful friends are trying to secure the vacant Mexican Mission for J. Maurice Thompson of Crawfordsville, Ind. J. Maurice Thompson is a poet. If he can get an indorsement from E. C. Stedman, his chances of becoming Minister to Mexico will be good."

In 1892 or early in 1893 he became the owner, through his wife's inheritance, of a sedate and substantial mansion situation in the east end of Crawfordsville.[127] The family had previously lived in a rambling and comfortable house at 908 East Main. Sherwood Place, as he called his new home, was built about the middle of the century and stood in the center of a five-acre plot of "trees, grass, vines, flowers and birds."[128] It had a basement and two and one-half stories—nineteen rooms in all. It was an appropriate setting for the ideals of social grace to which he aspired.

In the last decade of his life, however, Thompson lived in considerable retirement from the town. The recollections of Crawfordsville residents indicate that he was very careful about his health during this period, but the quantity of work he was turning out would have left even a healthy man little time for socializing. In addition, his lectures and his winters in the South frequently took him out of town. This social withdrawal from the town gave rise to the feeling among some residents that the Thompsons were a snobbish family, which was probably not the case: Thompson was absorbed in his work, and his work was outside the town. Another factor was the satisfaction he derived from an unusually happy family life. "I'm so intensely domestic, am so happy in my home life that if I mention it I begin to feel eloquent."[129] This domesticity was intensified as his children began to reach maturity; hence most of the social functions at Sherwood Place were gatherings of young people.

Nevertheless, Thompson continued his close friendship with Lew Wallace, as well as contacts with other midwestern notables. Such men as James Whitcomb Riley and Charles Major were sometimes visitors to Sherwood Place; young Meredith Nicholson, too, knew Thompson fairly well, if we may judge by his account of the older man in *The Hoosiers*. And as a national literary figure, he certainly would have had contacts with the Wabash College faculty, for he was a frequent speaker there during the 1890's.

Living congenially in a strongly Republican milieu, it was perhaps inevitable that Thompson should eventually find himself opposed to the policies of the Democrats. His break occurred in 1896 when the Populists gained control of the party and campaigned for financial policies favorable to the debtor class, mostly the hard-pressed western farmers. In the last two campaigns of his life, Thompson supported William McKinley and expansion.

As the century drew to a close, then, Thompson presented the picture of a financially, socially, and professionally successful man. His position on the *Independent* was secure, and he enjoyed an impressive reputation, particularly in the Midwest and South. In the fall of 1900 his novel *Alice of Old Vincennes* headed for the best-seller list immediately upon publication, and by January of 1901 it was in first place according to the *Bookman*.

But Thompson lived only to realize this success, not to savor it. A photograph of him made in October, 1900, when he was 56, shows him looking thin and old. Early in December an attack of grippe prevented his going south at his usual time (about mid-December), and by early February hope for his recovery had been abandoned. He died of pneumonia early on the morning of February 15, in his own room at Sherwood Place, surrounded by his family.[130]

CHAPTER II

THE NATURALIST

DURING THOMPSON'S LIFETIME the people who knew him best thought of him primarily not as a novelist or poet or even a critic, but rather as a nature-lover and a nature-writer. Lew Wallace, his partner on many a hunting and fishing trip, said, perhaps a little extravagantly, that Thompson courted nature "with the fine spiritualism of a poet who had eyes to see her material glories, splendors of the day and night, and also eyes of the soul to look into her mysteries and analyze them, and make them parts of himself, and enjoy as well as worship them."[1] One of his colleagues on the *Independent* (probably William Hayes Ward) wrote in a short introduction to Thompson's last contribution to the magazine (an account of a two-week camping trip on the Salliquoy River) that the piece was "characteristic of his best genius in its choicest field."[2] Mary Hannah Krout wrote in her memorial to Thompson of his hatred of cities and his "passionate love for the woods and fields. . . . His most exquisite verse is the poetry of streams and forests."[3]

A generation after his death, in spite of the popularity of *Alice of Old Vincennes,* Thompson was still well remembered as a naturalist.[4] There was reason for this opinion, if one surveys his writings. Although his seven volumes of essays and poems—devoted largely to nature subjects—are not an impressive total against his twelve volumes of fiction, still the nature motif in the fiction is strong, and sometimes obtrusive. And his uncollected periodical contributions—roughly 625—are approximately one-third nature essays. This does not include his uncollected poetry, about one hundred items,

of which roughly three-quarters is devoted to nature themes. None
of the writers mentioned above suggested that Thompson's experiences in the woods and his attitudes toward nature were in any
way related to his criticism of literature and society, but since I
believe this to be the case, his nature experiences and nature
writings require discussion here.

As A. O. Lovejoy has shown, the term "nature" in literary
usage often has a protean quality. For Thompson, it meant both
the wilderness environment, untouched by man, and the agrarian
environment of the rural South and Midwest. It is contrasted
always to the urban and the industrial. As a primitivist, again to
follow Lovejoy, Thompson is both "hard" in his commitment to
the wilderness values and "soft" in his feeling for the Arcadian
qualities of agrarian life.

Like all the literary primitivists of the eighteenth and nineteenth
centuries, Thompson conceived of nature, whether wild or Arcadian, as a refuge from the degenerative influences of "civilization."
It was a realm to which he could escape for incomparable sensuous and emotional pleasures which at once restored and strengthened a body weakened by civilized living; and it fertilized and
freshened an imagination jaded by the demands made on it for
earning a dollar. Nature was a refuge from society. He also regarded it vaguely as the basis of his esthetic, although he was never
able to work out the relationship in specific terms.

The sensuous and emotional pleasure which Thompson took in
nature is perhaps best described as a sophisticated atavism. It was
not unique with him; Thoreau's savage urge to devour a wood-
chuck raw is an example of it. But Thompson carried it to an
extreme nowhere else evident in American writers. Whereas
Thoreau, and to a lesser degree John Burroughs, intellectualized
their experiences with nature, Thompson only rarely did, and he
made a marked effort to intensify the emotional and sensuous
qualities of his experience and to enjoy them fully because of their
absence in his civilized life. This atavistic delight appears as an
elemental and irrational joy, sometimes almost an ecstasy, like
the "quiet wing-tremblings of delight" which he saw in certain
birds.[5] Its sources were myriad: the wind or the wash of the
warm Gulf waves over his naked body; the sight of three brown-
flecked eggs lying in a nest, bringing a smile to his lips and a
surge of inexplicable emotion in his breast; the sudden rise of

a bird from cover, sending him off in exultant pursuit before he could consciously realize what was happening; the twang of his bow cord, or the solid "chuck" of an arrow as it impaled or bowled over a bird; the first bite of a broiled meadow-lark's thigh, bringing a gush of saliva into his mouth; the taste of a paw-paw, a bud, a leaf, or a piece of bark, which he frequently nibbled during his excursions.

Although this atavism runs through his nature essays, its purest expression, and one of the most appealing essays that Thompson ever wrote, is his account of three weeks spent with an Indian named Tommy among the streams, marshes, and inlets of Florida's Indian River. The essay has a Melvillian smack—Melville among the Typees, except that Fayaway is conspicuously absent. The narrative begins when Thompson and his gear are dropped into Tommy's frail pirogue from a trader's schooner somewhere in the shark-infested waters of San Lucie Sound. The boat leaps away under the powerful strokes of the Indian, and, with each stroke, the white man sheds a bit of his civilized veneer. The first morning, they dramatically and skillfully fill a catamount full of arrows, and "over its body we silently welded our new-born friendship; . . . henceforth our mutual confidence was firmly established. . . . This savage sportsman was in an instant dearer to me than all the enlightened men who had ever laughed at what they were pleased to call my 'medieval crotchet.'" For the next three weeks life fluctuates between the two extremes of savage existence; the taut intensity, the physical danger, and the exultation of the chase, as in the death of the catamount; and the infinite, careless, rapturous ease that follows. "Lying on the white sand of the beach, I felt time drift by me, like a fragrant tide, every moment a bubble and every hour a warm, foamy wave of quiet joy. . . . Ah, what a lover salt sea water is! it embraces one all over, and thrills him through a thousand nerves to his remotest marrow." Taken all together it meant meeting "Nature face to face and [putting] your hand against her cheek. . . ."

When he comes to the end of the trip, there is real pathos in the parting. He is boosted aboard the trader's schooner by a very stolid Tommy who says merely, "'Ugh, Goodby,'" and they fly apart, "like two sea-birds," the white man wondering a little uncertainly if, after all, the savage wasn't just a trifle glad to get rid of him. It is one of the rare instances in which Thompson succeeds markedly in getting his reader's sympathy.

Curiously, there is no hint on Thompson's part of the squalor or discomfort of the savage life. It is the trader who remarks, "The dirtiest, greasiest, outdaciousest-looking man in the world you are!" when he gets him aboard the schooner.[6]

The beneficial practical effects of this delight in atavism extended also to the less intense pleasures of contact with nature. Outdoor exercise generated "sound lungs, healthy blood, a good appetite and a clear brain,"[7] all necessary preliminaries to a sound and whole view of life; and there was as well a mystical, inexplicable effect working through the imagination. Thompson's statement of it has an Emersonian tang: "What sweet and sure alchemic recipes Mother Earth gives us, if we could but read them! How unfailing are her schemes for the perpetuation of life, freshness, strength, beauty!"[8]

There was something particularly potent about water to him. Streams and brooks were the axes on which the world of nature revolved, so to speak. Water was "the finest type of material splendor, mobility, grace, action: and while we gaze it reflects, foreshadows, and etherealizes everything. It is the great purifier of earth, air and life. . . . All nature tends towards the streams."[9] This ineffable attraction of water was no doubt part of the appeal that fishing held for him. He said as much when he asserted that "a current of ancient vigor, the original elixir of nature flows with a bass brook; you feel its dew-like freshness go over you like the spirit of Greek poetry as soon as you begin to wade."[10] Essentially the same appeal went with the long bow, with the addition, however, of a "poetic" aspect deriving from the most ancient times. It "may well be termed the poet's weapon," he said. "The delight of it! The refreshment of it! The deep reach of it in the wells of pure imagination! And here is the significance of my bow and quiver: they satisfy the imagination and energize, recreate, the primitive man in me."[11]

Optimism, too, was to be derived from contact with nature. Even after a harrowing night under a rock ledge with a rattlesnake for a companion, the clear light of morning and the song of the mockingbird "wove their spell of optimism around me."[12] Fishing generated it: an honest angler "charges himself so thoroughly with all that is fresh in Nature during the season of verdure and warmth, he so brims his mind and his heart with joy, that he is perforce a jocund optimist all the rest of the year."[13] But nature required of her devotees that they approach her humbly and without self-consciousness, bent on recreation alone. Only then would she give herself, as to a lover. It was in this respect that Thoreau failed, according to Thompson, and thus missed the great lesson that nature had to teach. "He looked into himself instead of into external nature. Outdoor life was not recreation to him; it was his labor, his business. [One] must not, as Thoreau did, become an egotist and a posturer—a mere self-conscious meddler— in nature's presence. He would better be her playfellow, and thus throw her off guard, and win her secrets while she is not suspecting him."[14]

This crotchety and ill-founded judgment tells more about Thompson than about Thoreau, namely, that he was unnaturally concerned with keeping his "nature" as a place of refuge safe from probings by the intellect; and, taken with his tendency to describe nature experiences in terms of human love imagery (a wave "embraces one all over"; he puts his hand "familiarly against her cheek"), it suggests that nature experiences were also outlets for certain suppressed drives in Thompson's personality.

In a more general sense, his nature activities also served as a symbolic escape into a prewar Arcadia. All his activities were colored by a nostalgia for the values, if not for the forms, of this prewar life, and his nature activities particularly were associated with what appeared in retrospect to be a wonderfully free and joyful existence. The appeal of Bay St. Louis was undoubtedly related to this nostalgia. This quiet cultural backwater not only supplied ample opportunities for contact with nature but also presented a social scene that retained a strong flavor of the antebellum days.

As a nature writer Thompson was not *sui generis*. He had done a respectable amount of reading in the literature of ornithology and of natural science in general—he mentions such names as Darwin, Wallace, Huxley, A. Milne-Edwards, March, Gray, Coulter, Seeley, Coues, as well as more literary writers like Burroughs, Torrey, and Mrs. Miller—and of course the standard library of bird lovers: the works of Buffon, Gilbert White, Alexander Wilson, and Audubon. So it was not unnatural that with such examples he should fall into theorizing about the processes of nature, attempting to give some kind of systematic form to his observations.

His speculations about birds led him into assertions that range from the profoundly perceptive to the bizarre and the contradictory. He could, for example, deride the sentimental idea that bird song is a paean of praise to the Creator, and elsewhere sentimentally imagine that a bluebird was saying to him, "John Burroughs sends his greetings."[15] He could deride the theory of "dry-as-dust professors" that bird song has an erotic basis and then elsewhere describe the rare dropping song of the mockingbird with the conclusion, "My point was made: I had discovered beyond question that the dropping-song was a love-lyric," as though it were a new idea that he was advancing.[16] He believed that birds have personalities: that the shrike has a furtive, criminal look on his face when he is stalking a victim; that the mockingbird is temperamentally inclined to optimism and at times sings consciously with the object of gaining the favor of his human neighbors.[17]

His theories about the development of birds appear very doubtful to the present-day mind, although they might not have been so bizarre to his contemporaries, who, if they were philosophically inclined at all, were strongly influenced by the system of Herbert Spencer and John Fiske. Thompson's ideas lean toward the Lamarckian position, with a strong dash of pure imagination. For example, his theory that birds have hereditary memory, which accounts for their ability to return to the same place every year in migration and which enables a kingfisher, say, to transmit to his descendants his memories about a certain stream that he has thoroughly explored. Another of Thompson's theories was that birds undergo structural changes through the influence of "natural desire," i.e., that when the environment makes a certain change in bodily structure necessary for survival, then the intuitive natural desire of the bird for the change in structure will, in the course of a few generations, bring it about—a kind of mind-over-matter theory.[18] Unfortunately he was so unwary as to get tangled up with absolute value judgments in this process: the question of "pure" and "degenerate" species. He described the ivory-billed woodpecker as the "original type of the woodpecker, and the one pure species left to us in America," and all other species as "degenerate" offshoots of this original.[19] Such a distinction of course implies questions which he did not notice, and this very oversight is an index of his inability to get outside the realm of emotion and value judgment, even in science. It is a further indication of his necessity to refer everything to a supernatural orientation, which is precisely what he did in his next step of theorizing.

This concerned the question of how birds fly—a question of no small interest in that period when man had not yet managed to get himself off the ground except by lighter-than-air machines. Although Thompson came nearer to the facts than did some of his contemporaries—he saw the problem as one of explaining the bird's incredible muscular endurance, and he treated derisively the theory that birds have air sacs in their bodies and bones by which they make themselves as light, or lighter than, air—he still had to refer the problem to the Almighty. He took his motto for the essay from Richard Hooker: "There is no faculty or power in creatures which can rightly perform its functions without the perpetual aid of the Supreme Being."[20] A further indication of his retreat from the rational in his approach to ornithology was his distinction between ornithology and the "science of bird-loving." The latter, he said, "is to the more practical study what religion is to biology— the explanation of the unexplainable."[21] The parallel fails to hold up under logical scrutiny, but the statement of it serves to show Thompson's tendency to fall back on the faith of his fathers when confronted by a problematical situation.

In this, however, he was more typical than atypical of his generation, even of that liberal segment that had received its first solid intellectual aliment from preachers like Henry Ward Beecher and philosophers like Herbert Spencer and John Fiske. The *Independent* was known as a liberal religious magazine. Thompson numbered himself among the religious liberals and expressed at times a gentle contempt for those less enlightened persons who could not reconcile Genesis and geology. (At other times he called the attempt at reconciliation "blasphemous.")

There is strong presumptive evidence that in his theorizing he owed a great deal to Spencer and Fiske, especially in his version of evolution. We have already seen the Lamarckian tendencies (a part of Fiske's system) in his remarks on the development of birds. As for the development of nature as a whole, Thompson believed that it is guided "by God's law, bounded by His limiting purpose." And again, "The more I have studied nature the more I have become aware of God."[22] If anything, Thompson's God was more awesome, and definitely more personal, than Fiske's. God is unapproachable: "No analysis of the specialist, no synthesis of the generalizer can ever pass beyond the vail [*sic*]. God said: 'Let life be,' and life was. . . . When we study Nature we study Him, not in the materialistic or pantheistic sense, but in the Christian sense. The will of the universe is God's will. . . . Geology tells me the same story that Moses and the prophets tell me. . . ."[23] There is, however, a divine inspiration which we must accept without question above and independent of that human inspiration which we can feel from the study of nature.[24] As we shall soon see, this distinction was troublesome to him when he attempted to think through the relation of science and religion.

Such opinions as these show Thompson edging toward a basic difference from Fiske and Spencer—a difference which appeared in the distinction between divine and human inspiration. Another basic difference is that he made no attempt to explain the purpose or direction of the evolutionary process. That would be not only sacrilegious but also destructive of all the "romance" and interest of living. He implied elsewhere, possibly without intending to, that the task may be insuperable because there may be no plan. This lapse grew out of the need to defend himself against the charge of incongruity and contradiction in certain of his essays. He pled the example of nature: "Nature is incongruous, nay more, it is contradictory, as are certain of my essays. At one time my observations of facts clearly prove one thing; at another time they certainly establish just the opposite thing. I am not sure that this is altogether my fault, for Nature is tricksy in her moods. . . . She strings her creations together without rhyme or reason."[25]

Possibly another factor that puzzled Thompson when he came to look for plan or pattern in nature was his abundant knowledge of the Darwinian struggle. Although he never went so far as to find nature "red in tooth and claw," he did point out that "when I am hungry for bird-flesh, let the bird beware, as the worm and the butterfly must beware of the bird, as the wren must dodge the shrike."[26] This describes order of a sort, but because it is an amoral order it was intolerable to Thompson's temperament. To bring this Darwinian order within an intellectual synthesis, he turned back to the "romantic" (an extremely vague term in his usage) to justify it. Perhaps the following statement is his most significant expression of a basic attitude toward the problem of plan or purpose in nature: "To me all nature is romance; even the skull of a bird is the flower of a long *chanson de geste* coming up through a million years of adventure and change from the fish or the saurian. Every species of plant or animal has an heroic significance when I remember what a battle it has fought for existence."[27] This is one of Thompson's most interesting feats of intellectual gymnastics: by seeing "romance" and heroism in the Darwinian struggle, through a purely connotative process, he made it moral, and hence acceptable.

The "romantic" element, in a different sense, attracted Thompson equivocally to pantheism. In "The Threshold of the Gods," an essay that is, from a technical point of view, one of his finest achievements,[28] he flirted with pantheism but finally denied it because the state of civilization in his time, .i.e., Trinitarian Christianity, had carried men beyond the possibility of such belief. Nevertheless, the poetic, imaginative appeal of pantheism was very great for him—it was only because it was immoral (irreligious) that he was impelled to resist it.

The strength of this religious commitment was finally apparent when he attempted to think out a satisfactory relationship among art, science, and religion. He insisted upon the separate existence of the human soul and the value of its aspirations, under the guidance of Christianity, toward fuller development and realization of itself. Science should work entirely apart from this spiritual process. In all the discussion of whether science and revelation are compatible there is a "ring of blasphemy. Let science go on enlightening our minds and let Christianity go on making glorious the paths of men. There is room and great need for both. Walking between the two, with a hand on the shoulder of either, let poesy gather the bird-songs and perfumes of all the woods and fields from the beginning to the end of time."[29] The obvious intent of this metaphor was to bring these divergent tendencies into some sort of significant relationship, and purely as an image, it may have its appeal. But its meaning begins to blur on close examination. "Poesy's" hand on the shoulder of either remains nothing more than that; science and religion are just as far apart as ever, and the relation of "poesy" to them is not at all clear.

It should be apparent by now that Thompson was not at his best in the area of conceptual thinking, that his habits of thought and expression were metaphorical to a marked degree, and that his metaphors, though sometimes striking, were not always logically successful. That conflicting demands, both emotional and intellectual, were at work on his mind is plain enough: his loyalty to his paternal (and maternal) religion was sorely strained by the intellectual demands of agnostic and materialistic science a la Huxley and by the appeal of a Unitarian dilution of this science in the manner of Fiske. It was an intolerable situation from which there was really no refuge, but, being only human, he sought to find one—first, in confident assertions which were not always consistent with each other or within themselves and second, in a belief in the importance of "romance" (probably best defined in this particular context as the inexplicable) as the element which makes life tolerable and even exciting. The result of this emotional tension was that Thompson's moods were fully as "tricksy" as those he purported to find in nature.

All this may seem very far from the discussion of Thompson as a nature writer, and in a strict sense it is. But an understanding of the man behind the pen will help to illuminate his achievements and his failures as a writer not only of nature essays but of fiction, poetry, and criticism as well.

It is not easy to break down for orderly discussion Thompson's wide-ranging activities as a naturalist, because he did not keep them separate in his lifetime. His archery was as much ornithology as archery, his explorations a combination of all his interests. There are no "periods," unless his four years as state geologist of Indiana, 1885-89, could be so described. Geographically his activities extended from southern Florida and the Gulf Coast between Tampa and New Orleans to the Leelanau peninsula of northern Michigan. He began in the hill country of Georgia, went to Okefenokee Swamp and Lake Okeechobee and Indian River, then to the Midwest, where during his railroad experience between the Ohio River and the Great Lakes he was incidentally enjoying his nature studies. In 1872 he was able to say that he had studied the sapsucker from Georgia to "the Northern Lakes," probably meaning Erie or Michigan.[30] It is doubtful that he had been as far north as upper Michigan before 1877, the date he gave in a pair of travel sketches written four years later.[31]

After he was settled in Crawfordsville, he often returned to the Georgia hill country and also occasionally to Okefenokee. For instance, he told of a visit to Copse Hill, the home of Paul Hamilton

Hayne, in November, 1881, after a fortnight alone in Okefenokee. And numerous sketches, as well as some of his novels, attest to his familiarity with the North Alabama hill country, northwestern Florida, and the Mississippi Gulf Coast. He apparently began spending his winters in Bay St. Louis about 1884-85. His first magazine contribution dated from there was in January, 1886, but he recorded killing a fine specimen of the ivory-billed woodpecker "early in January, 1885, in a swamp near Bay St. Louis." The *Critic* also printed a letter from Bay St. Louis dated December, 1884.[32] These winters on the Gulf Coast marvelously extended his opportunities for bird study—especially for study of the mockingbird, a peculiarly deep and lasting interest with him—as well as for his explorations in the marshes, bayous, and swamps that extend from the Pearl River westward almost to New Orleans, an area of abundant wild life.

After 1885, Thompson divided his time between Crawfordsville and Bay St. Louis. He retreated, as the cold closed in over Indiana, to the near-spring weather of the Gulf Coast winter, and advanced again the following spring to spend the summer and fall in Indiana.

His summers in Crawfordsville offered a wide range of experience. Every afternoon, if the weather permitted, there was some kind of outdoor exercise: archery in the yard, or an hour or two with a bass rod on Sugar Creek, or a run into the country on his bicycle, often with his bow along.[33] The grove which sheltered Sherwood Place was a refuge for numerous birds which Thompson spent many hours studying.[34]

The Kankakee region of Indiana and Illinois was also a favorite haunt. The broad river with its marshy, wooded boundaries was ideal for both fishing and hunting. During his later years he and Lew Wallace used a steam-driven houseboat on the river for their excursions.[35]

Considering the fact that Thompson was called an ornithologist in his own day, one finds a surprisingly small amount of what might be called ornithological studies, and among modern ornithologists his name is hardly known. His principal undertaking was the dissection and study of the vocal or singing apparatus of some hundreds of birds with a view to determining how bird song is produced.[36] But basically his bird studies were nonscientific. The actual field work was done as recreation, and the use he made of the material was imaginative, poetic, belletristic. There are indications that he had collected a considerable amount of data with the intention of eventually publishing a serious ornithological work, but it never appeared and the fate of the notes is unknown.[37]

Of his work as state geologist of Indiana there is little to say. His appointment was greeted with general surprise, and at his death one commentator was candid enough to admit that not much had been expected of him in the office. Nor did he produce much: a total of eighteen items in three different departmental reports. All but two were on structural and historical geology, the exceptions being one on the bird life and one on the plant life of the Kankakee region.[38]

Perhaps his most lasting influence as a naturalist was on a group whose interest in nature per se was only marginal—the archers. The archery sketches which he began publishing in 1873 led to the publication, in 1878, of *The Witchery of Archery* and to the establishment in 1879 of the National Archery Association, of which he was the first president. In 1926 Robert P. Elmer, the first thorough historian of American archery, said that Thompson's "wonderful little book . . . had as much effect on archery as 'Uncle Tom's Cabin' had on the Civil War."[39]

When Thompson began one of his essays, "As for me, open the door and let me out. The wind will blow me to a lodgment in paradise; the birds will call me to a blissful nook in joyland; and after I have been there you shall hear from me—it is inevitable,"[40] he was indulging in an accurate, if obvious, piece of self-analysis—particularly in his last remark. His habits of note-taking and sketching kept his experiences on tap, as it were, for later reworking; and whatever it was (beyond the need for an income) that drove him to literary expression also enabled him to find in his nature experiences a large proportion of his subject matter. His poetry, his fiction, and his critical essays draw constantly on his nature lore for ideas, metaphors, and illustrations. But it is his nature essays, strictly speaking, that concern us here.

Like his nature activities, his nature essays are not easily compartmentalized. Fishing, bowshooting, bird study are mingled, apparently with very little conscious thought as to effect. Literary allusion is frequent, sometimes obtrusive, and sallies into literary and social criticism occur at quite unexpected times, particularly in those essays written toward the end of his life. His mode of organization is associative—"intuitive," he would call it, or "imaginative." For instance, when he started out to write about the shrike, the mention of Buffon's essay on that bird diverted him into a biographical sketch of Buffon with animadversions on Buffon's critics and eventually into a brief survey of a good part of Buffon's writings.[41] Or in describing his attempt to shoot a heron in a Mississippi swamp, he digressed into an anecdote about an old friend who was shot at by an Indian, and thence to Roger Ascham and *Toxophilus*.[42] These examples are representative, not exceptional: what unity the essays have is usually a unity of tone rather than of material or structure.

Perhaps Thompson realized this (maybe not even consciously), for it was as a stylist, in a very narrow sense, that he excelled. Part of his appeal to the readers of his time, of course, was in the material, the ideas. Even now there are few Americans who cannot be reached to some degree by a nostagically presented Arcadia. Any issue of *Sports Afield* or *Field and Stream* furnishes abundant evidence of the perennial appeal of such material. But Thompson's peculiar appeal was stylistic, for he was an informal and personal essayist in the fullest sense of the term. Charles Lamb and Thomas De Quincey, especially the latter, were favorites of his, and their influence, as well as that of Montaigne, is apparent in his work.[43] Thompson was cognizant of the dramatic element in the work of all these writers. He pointed it out in Montaigne and gave his highest praise for De Quincey to that writer's "Vision of Sudden Death," probably the most dramatic piece De Quincey ever wrote. This appreciation for the dramatic is obvious in his own essays, in spite of his tendency to divagation. He set his persona on the stage, and then with humor and sometimes with pathos traced the movements of this persona as the chief actor in a closet drama. The literary ego is revealed as impulsive, non-conformist, often insouciant (especially toward realists, rural clods, and dry-as-dust professors), and given to escape into the realms of the imagination. All in all, Thompson managed to paint himself as an interesting and amusing person, if sometimes crotchety and not quite lovable in his dogmatism.

Syntactically Thompson's style is vigorous, rather plain, clear, compact sometimes to the point of sententiousness, and on the whole well-adapted to the recounting of observations and simple action in a humorous minor key. The dramatic tension is maintained in the economy and terseness of the expression; it suffers only from structural faults, his tendency to digress. Terseness and economy are particularly noticeable in the essays devoted principally to fishing and archery. In reporting dialogue, however, which is not infrequent in these essays, his control sometimes slipped when he was handling characters who would be expected to have social status—usually himself and his brother. The result is a pompous, overly genteel, and thoroughly unnatural mode of speech. But in reporting the language of characters without social status—Negroes, crackers, mountaineers, and Hoosier clods—he achieved an excellent effect of naturalness and raciness, as good as the best of Augustus Baldwin Longstreet or George Washington Harris.[44] Compare, for instance, this stilted exchange between the brothers with the ease and naturalness of a Florida hermit's speech:

" 'How hungry one gets with a few hours' fast in the open air!' said Will, munching a cracker. 'How delightfully aggravating the smell of broiling bacon! I believe this sort of life has a tendency to make an animal of a man! Why, it's all I can do to restrain an impulse now to whinny for my food like a hungry horse!'

" 'And the coffee, too,' said I, feeling the fascination of the subject—'and the coffee, too, sends out a most persuasive odor.' "[45]

Now hear the hermit, who has just discovered a long black twist of Old Virginia in the possession of their Negro servant: " 'That's the docyment,' cried the man delightedly, 'That's the docyment, darkey. We'll jest divide this 'ere weed right here.' " And after depositing a large quid in his jaw he adds, " 'That's the cl'ar stuff, darkey, cl'ar stuff. Thanky, boy, thanky.' "[46]

The personal, and hence the dramatic, element is a little less marked in the bird studies, but here, too, the sentence structure retains the directness and ease that adds so much to the hunting and fishing descriptions. When Thompson wrote of birds there is a noticeable difference in diction, a tendency toward the poetic, imaginative, suggestive, which gets its fullest play in an essay that for its combination of unusual features deserves separate consideration.

"The Threshold of the Gods" is a piece almost worthy of Poe or De Quincey, and it has affinities with both.[47] Thompson's aim was to advance what he called his "grove theory" of the origin of belief in the gods of pagan mythology, the substance of the theory being that in the virgin condition of the forests, unknown and now unknowable elements existed which could cause in a person of imaginative temperament a kind of quasi-hallucination, a fleeting and half-certain glimpse of the "spirit" of a grove or a fountain. In itself, the theory would hardly get a passing notice, but the method he adopted to present it shows a control of form which he never attained again. The vehicle is a trip down a mountain river and through rapids bordered on one side by a granite escarpment and on the other by virgin forests. During the trip he skillfully introduced at intervals a series of themes, returning to them again and again, and developing them finally into a unified climax. First there is the halcyon, the belted kingfisher, sounding his "idiot's chuckle," flying leisurely from tree to tree ahead of the pirogue, and increasing his pace with the speed of the current and the boat: he functions as a kind of guide-spirit. Next there is the motif of the lowering twilight, eventuating in near-darkness at the climax. Then comes the approach—slow at first, but increasingly fast—to the beginning of the rapids, which are marked by a luminous line of water and a rift in the forest along one bank. After each of these motifs has been introduced, returned to, and developed, he is ready for the climax:

> We slipped on and on, still following the now madly careering halcyon. For the merest point of time, not long enough for an eye to twinkle, we were opposite the rift in the woods and trembling on the verge of mystery. I looked down the open vista and saw something, I know not what—a form or a shadow, an image conjured up by my imagination, or only a blending of the glooms and gleams by force of distance and velocity—but a new element was added to my nature. I felt a great thrill. A new joy took root in my heart. A new flower blew open in my soul. . . .
>
> It seemed that down that aisle I could look to the remotest age of time; and out of it, blowing into my eager face, I felt the unchanged, the unchangeable spirit of Eld! Was it, or not, a face that I saw? Can I ever know? The flowing hair, like blown supple ringlets of gold floss, the gray deep eyes, the divinely smiling lips; were they not there? And the shining body and agile limbs, did I only fancy I saw them? How shall I ever be sure? *O! Dea certe.* An indescribable something, as of that whole landscape melting and vanishing, by a sudden and noiseless deflagration, followed close upon this fortunate moment. With a harsh, maniacal cry of delight, the belted halcyon leaped over the coruscating line into the silvery mist beyond. And, like an arrow flung from the bent bow of the river, we were whirled after him into the vast fanged jaws of the cañon.[48]

The dramatic intensity of this excerpt is typical of bits of Thompson's best work—never a whole essay—but the other obvious quality, that of suggesting rather than stating the idea, is one that requires a lightness of touch that he did not often achieve. The structure of the essay as a whole, too, shows a striking contrast to his usual formlessness, the implication being, I believe, that he was not insensitive to structure—he could achieve it when he wanted to—but generally found his associative method of organization more appropriate to the personal, informal, insouciant tone of most of the essays. Of course there is also the possibility that he was reluctant or lacked time to take the pains to achieve structure and balance, since there is nothing in these qualities that is necessarily destructive of an informal tone.

Thompson's reputation as a nature writer was considerably greater during his lifetime than it has been since his death. Even so, the relatively enthusiastic reception of his first nature book, *The Witchery of Archery,* did not extend to any of his subsequent books. As far as critical acclaim is concerned, he started near the top of the ladder and worked down.

Perhaps one of the reasons for the critical notice of the first book was the popularity of archery just at that time and the admitted part that Thompson had played in bringing it about. Howells reviewed the revised edition for the *Atlantic,* and although his comment was not effusive, it reflects solid approval. He pointed out the combination of "knowledge and inspiration, . . . fresh and original observation" that went into the book, and had particular praise for "The Death of the White Heron," a poem which Thompson later included in both collections of his verse. But it is praise which Thompson must have read with a pang: Howells, with the best heart in the world, called the poem "A marvelously genuine bit of poetic realism."[49]

The *Nation's* reviewer called *The Witchery of Archery* "a sensible little book" and forecast success for it, "in spite of its touch of claptrap in the title." *Scribner's* (whose parent organization was the publisher of the book) noted that "this pretty little volume is one of the few for which there is a genuine and not a fictitious 'demand'" and described the author as "an alert observer, a bold, vigorous, and poetic writer." The *Lippincott's* reviewer avowed himself bewitched and amply demonstrated it by devoting most of the review to his own opinions and experiences with the sport. *Harper's* jumped on the bandwagon by pointing out that one of the chapters first appeared in that magazine. All agreed that the style was striking and described it variously as "buoyant," "dramatic," "breezy." They likewise agreed that Thompson's close observation and sprightly description added greatly to the book's appeal.[50] On the whole it was a very friendly reception and must have been extremely encouraging to a young attorney for whom literature was still an avocation.

By-Ways and Bird Notes was published by John B. Alden in the fall of 1885 in a much less pretentious form than the preceding book. It also received much less notice than *The Witchery of Archery;* the *Critic* was the only important national magazine to give it more than a cursory review (the editors, Joseph B. and Jeanette Gilder, were moderately good friends of Thompson by this date). The reviewer gave it high praise; he was especially interested in Thompson's tendency to mix nature study and literary criticism in such a way as to "happily combine humanity and nature." Thompson's work was also seen as symptomatic of a movement in modern literature toward a return to nature, a tendency for authors to strengthen both themselves and their writings by a greater familiarity with external nature.[51] The *Atlantic* gave the book a bare mention: "We are always, unfailingly glad to meet Mr. Thompson out-of-doors . . . ,"[52] the last adverb possibly suggesting that the reviewer was not particularly glad to meet him except when he wrote of nature. This may, in turn, indicate that Thompson's strictures on realism in general and Tolstoi in particular had by this time begun to pall on Thomas Bailey Aldrich, for although he was conservative, his conservatism was of a different brand from Thompson's, and he shared the Boston reverence for Tolstoi and for restraint in public expression.

The notice in the *Literary World* suggests the same qualified approval. The reviewer liked best the papers dealing with the early days in Georgia, specifically mentioning "A Fortnight in a Palace of Reeds." Of Thompson's experiments in mingling nature studies and literary criticism he said, "The paper on 'Out-door Influences in Literature' just misses of being an exceptionally fine one, suggesting the thought, as Mr. Thompson's work occasionally does, that he might do better with more painstaking and restraint."[53]

By the time that *Sylvan Secrets* was published in 1887 (also by Alden), only the *Critic* was faithful, and even that journal did not get around to reviewing it until February of 1889. On the whole it was a favorable review, but the objections to certain aspects of the book were rather firmly and fully stated: "When a writer is eager to proclaim that a live titmouse is more to his taste than a dead poet, and that a mocking bird 'makes him forget that ever there was a Shakespeare' it need surprise no one that he writes more adequately of the bird than of the bard."[54]

One can only speculate whether the coolness of the critics, or the reluctance of the publishers, or the urgency of his editorial duties (begun in 1889) had anything to do with it, but Thompson refrained from collecting any more of his nature essays until 1900, when *My Winter Garden* appeared. The presence among his manuscripts of two unpublished collections, "With Bow and Rod" and "Toxophilus in Arcadia" suggests that it was the reluctance of publishers.

The notice of *My Winter Garden* was wider than for *Sylvan Secrets,* though nothing to compare with that of the first book. Except for his own magazine, the opinions again reflect a qualified approval and for the same reasons. Both the *Dial* and the *Nation* liked his natural descriptions but shied away from his literary criticism. According to the latter his descriptions of southern birds were "really fascinating," and "the Gulf coast in winter has rarely been more happily described. [In natural descriptions] his powers of observation and expression are at their best; and in his own field Mr. Thompson's best is very good indeed." But there is a good bit on the debit side too. His literary criticism "lacks sincerity," his quotations from Meleager and his reflections on Keats and Tennyson "are there for effect." All in all, he would do well "to stick to studies of birds and flowers and Southern swamps and spare us such literary criticism as the essay on Theocritus."[55]

The *Independent,* which was committed to support of Thompson as a literary critic, admired the book without reservation: "This is Mr. Thompson's chosen field, and there is now no living nature writer who has such grace and charm as he. These essays are in Mr. Thompson's best vein, and for persons who are interested in outdoor life and who love nature as well as books we recommend this volume."[56]

On the whole, Thompson was treated more than justly in these reviews. His talents were adequately recognized, and he richly deserved the censure he received.

Apart from reviews of his books, Thompson was not without recognition as a naturalist during his lifetime. True, Horace Greeley, almost at the end of his life, scolded the young man for his foolishness about bows and arrows,[57] but in the main the public was appreciative. By the middle 1880's he was acknowledged by one commentator to be an important member of a group of writers, descended from Gilbert White and Thoreau, who were bringing new life into American literature through the literary treatment of bird studies. The others included Bradford Torrey, Olive Thorne Miller, and John Burroughs; and from a literary point of view, Thompson was judged the best of the lot. He showed less abandon to "nature as she is" than did Burroughs, and although, as a student of natural history, his powers were limited, his "literary sense is very fine and delicate, and his style pure and limpid as the running brook." This style, said the critic, would insure a cordial reception to anything he wrote, "for while others may be read for their subject's charm, many more will read his work for the way in which he tells whatever he finds to write of."[58]

In 1892, *Book News* carried a biographical sketch of Thompson as one of a series on well-known literary figures, asserting that "few writers, perhaps, excel him in the description and interpretation of outdoor nature."[59] At his death the various obituaries and tributes made much of his devotion to nature and his signal success in interpreting nature.[60] The verse tributes, one by James Whitcomb Riley and another by Lloyd Mifflin, were principally concerned with his nature-love. Said Riley,

> He *would* have holiday—outworn, in sooth,
>   Would turn again to seek the old release,—
> The open fields—the loved haunts of his youth—
>   The woods, the waters, and the paths of peace.

And Mifflin added,

> A hush is on the prairie's endless plain;
>   Silence within the South; in plashy meeds
>   The heron, lonely, stands within her weeds,
> And all our woodlands have a touch of pain.
> Farewell! O singer of the sylvan strain.[61]

Within a short time after Thompson's death, Frank Norris was taking note of the "Nature revival" in literature, but curiously, he failed to mention Thompson and attributed the revival to the work of Ernest Thompson Seton and his imitators. He saw the movement as "a return to the primitive, sane life of the country, . . . an unerring groping backward toward the fundamentals, in order to take a renewed grip upon life." The magazines of the 1870's and 1880's, he believed, were quite bloodless, "oppressed with the bug-bear of 'literature.' Outdoor life was a thing apart from our reading." But in the new literature "nature has ceased to exist as a classification of science, has ceased to be *mis*-understood as an aggregate of botany, zoology, geology, and the like, and has become a thing intimate and familiar and rejuvenating. . . ."[62] These comments reveal that Norris was ignorant of Thompson's work, but more important, they suggest that Thompson's persistent espousal of nature in literature during the last three decades of the century may have been seminal to some of his younger and better-known contemporaries, for Norris' ideas about the effect of the nature revival on literature are the ideas Thompson had been repeating for thirty years.

During the 1920's and 1930's, although Thompson was remembered by nature lovers, he was regarded by them as a marginal figure in the tradition of nature writing.[63] Perhaps his most sensitive treatment during this period was at the hands of Henry C. Tracy, who was properly appreciative of his stylistic excellence, of his imaginative freshness, and of his primitive, unphilosophical delight in nature but who also saw plainly that he was more a facile writer than a great naturalist in the manner of Thoreau or Burroughs.

The archers should not be forgotten in this account. Placing them at the close of the chapter may give it one of those happy endings of which Thompson was so fond, for their devotion has been unwavering. From an early anonymous squib in the *Atlantic,* recommending Thompson, George A. Hansard, and Roger Ascham as the three writers whose books must be on any archery club's shelf,[64] to Robert P. Elmer's labor of love in editing a new edition of *The Witchery of Archery* in 1928, successive generations of archers have turned to his little book for both instruction and delight.

CHAPTER III

THE CRITIC

As a critic Thompson dealt with both the literary and the social orders because he felt that the two were dynamically related. In the last three decades of the century a critic taking such a view had an abundance of issues with which to concern himself: the social and economic absorption of the Negro and the immigrant; the effects of industrial and urban growth; immorality in business; the plight of the farmer; scientific inroads on orthodox Christian belief; literary piracy owing to the lack of international copyright up to 1891; the rise of nationalism and imperialism; and the rise of realism and naturalism in literature.

In his critical comments Thompson showed himself to be a remarkable exemplar of genteel middle-class values, the values of that large segment of society which aspired to respectability and status in a social order which they believed to be the best the world had ever seen.

Behind Thompson's conviction that art and society were dynamically related lies the psychological theorem, "We grow like what we contemplate, not like what we affect to imitate." He expressed it elsewhere as "Down the centuries we grow toward what most delights us," insisting always on a distinction between the efficacy of the imagination and that of the intellect. "The fiber, the tissue, nay, the very nerve-fluid of the social body, is to be reached and educated by sweet persuasion applied to that strange source of all human progress, the imagination."[1]

The social application of the theorem appears more fully in his assertion that "if you plan to control men, you first captivate their imagination. Give me the key to a people's imagination and you may have the rest; I will lead them through nine crusades in spite of you." As evidence, he pointed to the sexual freedom of French society: "From the remotest period of her literary life, the prevalence of lewdness in her fiction has reacted on her social and political development so that a sound view of the relation of the sexes has been impossible to her people."[2] Only once did Thompson indicate that the imagination might not be the most potent factor in the determination of human events; but this one instance, oddly, was in direct contradiction to his usual thesis. In explaining why John Ruskin had no great effect on society he said, "The activities of life are, indeed, little influenced by the great abstract thinkers. This world is a material one, and, hate materialism, as we justly may, it is affected most by material forces." This lone contradiction does not signify that Thompson's faith in the imagination faltered; it is, rather, an example of his tendency to use any avenue of attack that promised immediate result when he was trying to tear down the case of someone he regarded as dangerous. In this instance he was alarmed by Ruskin's attack on capitalism.[3]

The question of the psychological effect of evil on the individual, and hence on society, Thompson discussed almost wholly in terms of physical debauchery. In one of his earliest critical essays he viewed the deaths of Poe, Baudelaire, Byron, Keats, and Shelley as the consequences of unwholesome physical indulgences resulting from unwholesome mental diets. The belief that great genius is closely allied to madness, he said, is so much twaddle; the truth is that great genius is closely allied to great passion, and when an individual, though a genius, indulges his "base passions" he dies, as he deserves to.[4] This idea Thompson never gave up; however, in later years he gave it a more specifically sexual application when discussing the tendency of French writers to suffer mental breakdowns. He cited the fact that Balzac, Baudelaire, and Maupassant all suffered varying degrees of mental deterioration, due, according to their friends, to the use of drugs and to overwork. But Thompson believed them victims of their imaginations. "Evil thinking is poisonous to the brain."[5]

This conviction of the psychological potency of evil brought him up against the rather thorny question of what to do about evil in art if, as he believed, art should be true to life. He concluded that the artist must not ignore the existence of evil: "The law of our civilization exacts, not that we shall avoid deep consideration of base life and its results, but that base life shall not be made a matter of delectation, . . . the *point d'appui,* the focus of influence." For that reason he felt that it is not permissible for the major characters of a piece of fiction to be "bad persons," since sympathizing with evil is dangerous and successful fiction demands that the reader sympathize with the major characters.[6]

Thompson's theory of artistic creation began with a belief in genius as something palpably different from talent, in art as something different from artisanship. Genius he defined as "the power by which one mind generates in another mind an unmanageable enthusiasm." Emerson and Poe he cited as the foremost American examples of it, as Darwin was among the English.[7] This definition in turn he related to Sir Philip Sidney's observation that "Art moveth one to do that which it doth teach," and it is the ability to inject this power in art that Thompson believed to be genius. When we come to inquire in more detail just what the qualities of genius are, there is a point beyond which we cannot pass. Such qualities as "the enquiring eye, the clever understanding, the sense of distance, time and force, the quick and sure imagination, the grasp of dramatic correlations"[8] we can recognize; but beyond these there is always something inexplicable about a work of genius. The critic can no more explain the "occult processes" of genius than the biologist can explain the subtle tricks of vegetable life.[9]

The distinction between artist and artisan seems to have grown out of the same mood, i.e., a distinction between the understandable and the inexplicable. In designing a literary work, one is an artist; in executing it, an artisan.[10] Any artisan can be a professor of rhetoric and discourse on the "art" of writing, but it is only the artist, the genius, who is capable of compassing the true art of writing, and his achievement is not one that can be dissected and explained in words.

A certain mark of the artist or genius, according to Thompson, is his unfailing return to nature "for the component ingredients of new and racy thoughts."[11] This is the secret of true art, he said. "It is not a cultivation of structure with a view to form-variations, but rather the sincere presentation of forms and colors as they have eternally existed in nature."[12] However, there is more to it than merely describing what we see in nature. "A clear distinction may be easily made between what is written merely about nature and what is distilled from nature in the alembic of genius."[13] "Nature," as indicated in the preceding chapter, meant for Thompson both the pastoral, agrarian countryside of Indiana and the wilderness.

If nature is the artist's schoolmistress, it might seem that scholarship and tradition have little place in the works of genius; Thompson said as much at odd times. For instance, he asserted that "there seems to be no difference, in final efficacy, between the crude song of the hind and the finished sonnet of the academician, when in each case genius floods the words with the racy sap of originality and the fine light of personal charm."[14] Or again, "I have never thought that scholarship could injure a poet; the harm comes when learning leads to self-consciousness in the high ecstasy of composition."[15] But more often he was reluctant to cut poetry free from the past, particularly when he began to fear that the outer defenses of Parnassus were being sapped by such "realistic" poets as Whitman and the dialect rimesters like Riley. Whitman's poetry he regarded at times as an unmistakable sign of decadence, and a little study of the matter led him to the conclusion that a broad grounding in world literature was necessary to the artist: "He is the truest genius who finds the broadest ground upon which to graze his imagination." In fact, the more Thompson thought about Whitman, the surer he was that "the line of masters standing hand in hand from here to Homer and Theocritus is a line of blue-blooded aristocrats, educated to their position and recognizing the badge of learning."[16]

This insistence on the efficacy of genius and nature on the one hand and the necessity for tradition and culture on the other demands, in some way, an attempt to reconcile the two, but Thompson never fully faced the problem. Instead he attempted to write it off with the unelaborated statement that "the true poet would if untrammeled always reach back and keep touch with his uneducated nature; but this reach must be through an atmosphere of culture."[17]

One of the greatest dangers to genius, Thompson felt, was science, with its accompanying spirit of materialism, analysis, "realism," agnosticism, and pessimism (he added socialism in some contexts). He could conceive no kinship between the mood of science and the mood of art and believed that "so soon as art is set to academic rule, it becomes mere artisanship."[18]

But how is genius to be recognized, how are the norms of art to be established—upon the word of an elect group, upon the *consensus gentium,* or upon the word of the inspired critic? At one time or another, Thompson suggested all of these possibilities. The "all-reaching appeal [of genius]," he said, "is never separable from the average conceptions of beauty and truth."[19] But when he came to draw a distinction between fame and popularity he said that "the flame on high" is the true gauge of what is best in art: "The criticism immanent in the elect must keep telling the public what is good and true. We must depend upon this high source of light, not upon mere popular preference." Three sentences later he said, "What the immanent taste of many generations of good judges has set apart for eternal glory may be safely taken as a measure of permanent values."[20] That the taste of many generations is required to estabilsh a norm is in a way a denial of the immanence of that taste. The implication would seem to be that taste is based on the collective approval of an elect group rather than on a divine or ideal principle.

Another requirement of great art, Thompson felt, is nationalism, in the sense that it should express the highest qualities of the national culture from which it springs. An art expressive of national life, he said, was not denied to cultures other than the American, but it was clear that the greatest art must be American because "our civilizaion is winnowed in a stronger wind, and disinfected by a more focal sunlight than come to the peoples of the other great continents." Christianity was the chief influence to which our civilization was indebted, and for that reason Americans could hope that they were entering "the era of true Christian art and literature, the era which is to give the world the . . . romance of the Christian religion."[21]

Thompson's conception of Christianity centered around a mood of Victorian humanitarianism, a faith in the orderly progress of the world toward a society in which personal freedom, the rights of property and "the greatest good for the greatest number" in terms of both spiritual and material welfare should all be harmonized. It was "distinct from church, priesthood, theology, and formal religion— . . . a mode of progress, a great mood of civilization, broadening, deepening, warming day by day."[22] In opposition to this Christianity was a complex of values not so easy to characterize in a phrase. In Thompson's mind the most appropriate and inclusive term would have been "materialism." He wrote once to R. W. Gilder, "Poor pity-deserving America! Sold out to realism and materialism and money-grabbing."[23] But he also called Tolstoi's radical Christianity "materialistic," so it is clear that it was a very broad and rich word for him—more a bad name than a logical category.

If the best art is that which expresses the values and aspirations of American Christian civilization, while through its fascination engendering those values and aspirations in the minds of the audience, Thompson said, it is logical to expect that criticism has a judicial function in the process. Our critics, he said, "are our sentinels calling from the watch towers, notifying us of the coming of good or evil. In a large degree they shape public sentiment. How important it is that they be patriots of perfect stamp, loving their own people better than all other peoples, their own country better than all other countries! How supremely necessary that they shall sympathize with the genius of their country's civilization and measure all things with a view to their country's lasting glory and honor!"[24] The Christian element is evident in his assertion that "since the Christian civilization is the best the world has ever had, it is the chief function of criticism to prevent any weakening of its substance by the introduction of evil elements, or to cast out such elements, once they have entered." At the same time he was careful to disclaim any desire to foist off "mere sentimental morality and mere vainglorious patriotism" on the population, or to impose any kind of legal censorship.[25] The protection of public taste, or the elevation of it, must be accomplished, insofar as it can be, through the intellectual approach, by education and persuasion. The most potent means is of course through the imagination, through art itself.

Behind this whole theory lies the assumption that human beings are creatures of choice and free will, that "we can consciously mold life, just as we can consciously mold art [and that] criticism should aim to mold life and art both at once."[26] This was such a common assumption of Thompson's time and class that it would hardly deserve mention were it not that the contradictory assumption of determinism appears in some of his criticism, as it does in some

of his fiction. While deploring the tendency of eastern editors to
force their taste upon provincial authors, he twice said that they
were not to blame for the unhappy situation, that they were
"merely the product of environment." And in attempting to dis-
count Brunetière's criticism he said, "It is not difficult to feel the
historical environment that has made M. Brunetière not only
possible but inevitable."[27] These denials of free will and responsibility are best understood as momentary lapses growing out of the
journalistic pressures under which Thompson worked. But they do,
in addition, suggest his sensitivity to the growing amount of determ-
inistic thought in the intellectual climate of his time.

Thompson's most enduring interest was the defense of "romance." Even before he left Georgia, before the question of realism
versus romance became important on the critical scene, he was
beginning to think about the problem, doubtless stimulated by the
controversy that was still going on in France and Britain after the
publication of *Madame Bovary* in 1857. In *Scott's* for December,
1867, he published an essay entitled "Imaginative Romance,"[28]
which adumbrated his later attitudes. Although he conceived of
romance at this period as having to do with the "misty regions of
the unreal" an attitude that he later reversed, he was already ada-
mant against the handling of unholy love in fiction. *La Nouvelle
Heloise* he judged a "great bad book," dangerous to the young, "un-
healthy from sheer rankness of passion, and in truth but slightly in
advance of heathen literature in a moral sense."

All of his critical writing is marked by strong emotion and a
tendency to attach different meanings at different times to some
of his terms. Still a pattern of sorts emerges. In general, romance
is the prose equivalent of Ideal poetry. It is variously defined as
"the translation of the meanings, the forces, and the possibilities
of life into literature," as the "story of the unattained, which is attainable by some form of heroism," or as "the process in fiction-
making by which life is expressed in its higher meanings. Mathe-
matically, it is life raised to a higher power. It is truth to life, as
life could be and would be were it used to the best advantage (in
the case of the evil character) and to the medium advantage (in
the case of the commonplace character), as shown in a work of
fiction."[29] Although the inclusion of commonplace characters does
not quite make sense in terms of life "raised to a higher power," a

general idea of what Thompson was getting at emerges from these quotations, namely, that romance is the representation of a better and attainable life, usually through the means of fiction—although he sometimes extended the term to include other forms of art as well. He further believed that its appeal is rooted in human nature: "We are sojourners in a world which offers nothing real that can satisfy our souls," he said in his early *Scott's* essay; and thirty years later, when the growing vogue for historical romance made it appear that the aberration of realism was corrected, he asserted, "It had to come; human nature in its deepest wells held what made certain the return of heroism and romance."[30]

As one might expect, the function of romance does not end with the presentation in art of a better life; it is dynamically related to society. "Public sentiment is now, always has been, and always will be, molded by romance. The romance of preaching, the romance of oratory, of graphic art, of poetry, of prose fiction, takes hold of the human heart and leads it."[31]

What are the details of this better life? Perhaps the most essential qualities of it are optimism and heroism. "Heroism," Thompson said, "lies in the line of duty, and duty grandly done is the keynote of every truly great work of fiction." And to optimism he could give no higher praise than to find it a quality of "the dearest name in literature": "Sir Walter Scott . . . was always a boy; he lived and died an open-hearted, optimistic, imaginative youth, loving, beloved and full of life's richest magnetism." Elsewhere he said ex cathedra, "Great minds are ever [optimistic], for the vigor of greatness does not permit pessimism." He also believed "that aesthetics and pessimism cannot blend together; therefore true art is necessarily optimistic."[32] If, as he said in his nature essays, contact with nature instills optimism, then nature and romance must be congenial. Although he did not specifically mention in relation to romance such other qualities as patriotism, religious faith, reverence for women, and economic and social ambition, their importance may be inferred from his practice in fiction, from his objection to their absence in realism, and from his general tendency to justify in his critical essays the values of the respectable, middle-class midwestern society in which he lived.[33] The better life did not include—and he was very specific about this—those values reflected in what he called "pseudo romance": the school of goody-goody didacticism on the one hand and the school of sensationalism, represented by H. Rider Haggard, on the other. If anything, the goody-goody writers were in his judgment more reprehensible than the sensationalists, because at least the latter did not intend their outlandish creations to be taken for truth. But the former writers did purport to tell the truth, although we all know, Thompson said, that "this history of the good little girl who came to be so sentimentally religious that she melted away into a sort of pathetic treacle for angel-bread is out of the bounds of all honesty."[34]

These are the values which romance must reflect, but there are certain other requirements which must be met before it can be called great fiction. Thompson deduced them, he said, from the practice of Shakespeare:

1. There must be a story to tell.
2. The story must introduce us to extraordinary people—not impossible people, but people whose circumstances and whose lives are able to engender powerful interest.
3. The story must be thoroughly well imagined and told with consummate skill.
4. The atmosphere of actual human life must be so artfully hung over all the scenes that we feel it, breathe it, and live in it while we read.
5. Every element of the story must be referable to the sources of human passion, aspiration, credulity, fancy, faith or manners. Nothing in it must be untrue to universal human possibilities, yet each dramatic crisis must turn on some extraordinary conjunction. The commonplace must not preponderate.
6. There must be absolute dramatic vision; without this the novel is a mere tale, the drama a mere play, the painting a lifeless transcript, the music a meaningless tinkle, the sculpture a form without suggestion.
7. Last comes style, which is the final stamp of the personality of genius. There is no such thing as a masterpiece without the presence of this indescribable preservative.[35]

Two of these elements need further explanation. "Absolute dramatic vision" is a term taken from Theodore Watts-Dunton's article on poetry in the ninth edition of the *Encyclopedia Britannica*, with which Thompson was familiar. It means the author's ability to submerge his own personality absolutely while creating a character, the ability to envision character and action in a manner unconditioned by the personal or lyrical impulse. As Watts-Dunton stated it, the possessor of absolute dramatic vision, Shakespeare for instance, or Sophocles, "does not work, but is worked by his imagination."

The last item, style, is never very definitely explained, in spite of the fact that Thompson devoted much space to it in *The Ethics of Literary Art*. His descriptions of it are almost always metaphorical: it is "the smile of meaning," "the bloom of vigor," "the character-beams of countenance," which in the best literature reflect "individuality, luminosity, sincerity and rosy health."[36]

The requirements that the atmosphere of actual human life be "hung" over the scenes of great fiction and that no character or situation transcend the limits of human possibility posed for Thompson the question of the difference between romance and realism, since these attributes were claimed by others for realism. To answer the question Thompson made a distinction between true and "pseudo realism," dismissing the latter as the inferior art practiced by "realists" and identifying true realism as the "realism of romance." Under these terms he saw Balzac, whom the realists claimed as a literary forebear, as actually a romancer: "He deceived his readers at every turn; he makes black appear white; the impossible seems not only possible but inevitable; and by means of overwhelming details his romantic absurdities take on the form of commonplace events. . . ."[37]

Once, in attempting to distinguish between true and pseudo realism, he posited masculine and feminine principles. True realism, or romance, he identified with the masculine principle— virile, sweeping, concerned with large effects—and pseudo realism he associated with the feminine principle—delicate, limited, analytical.[38] Again, he attempted to explain the difference in terms of attitudes toward human nature, a distinction of no little perception, although his diction was extreme: "The only difference between realism and true romance in fiction is a difference in the appreciation of the nature and meaning of human aspiration. One deals with us as if we were animals to be subjected to vivisection; the other addresses itself to our humanity." Another potentially fruitful approach which he did not develop was the concept that realism is a "low order of romance, . . . romance conventionalized to suit a certain order of culture."[39]

But it is when he gets down to specific objections to realism that his significant attitudes begin to appear; it becomes apparent that to him "realism" was another bad name, the literary aspect of "materialism." He objected chiefly on moral grounds. Obsessed with a dual sense of the frailty of human nature on the one hand and of its heroic possibilities on the other, he saw realism as the worst of influences on both possibilities. Even when not dealing in outright vice, realism put stress on the foibles and peccadilloes of character—the commonplace aspects—"instead of attempting to imagine noble instances of human self-sacrifice, of lofty aspiration, of soul-stirring passion." "Will the soul," he asked, "grow beyond the stature of its model?" If daughters and wives read with delectation a book like *Anna Karenina,* he argued, you may know but too well what to expect from them. And they will read it with delectation, if they read it, because "art, like life, has its mighty temptations: The forbidden fruit is very red and ripe and inviting. Men long for it, as they long for all manner of fascinating evil."[40]

He categorically denied the allegation that certain realistic books that deal with vice may carry a moral. Such a theory is based, he said, on the palpably false assumption that handling dirt makes the hands clean. To one woman's objection that she had not found "a filthy phrase, a coarse allusion or a lewd remark" anywhere in *Hedda Gabler* (which Thompson had been attacking for its obscenity), he replied, "Here is the hopeless symptom of the case. My correspondent cannot feel or see the difference between intrinsic and extrinsic obscenity. She . . . cannot understand that artistically sugar-coated phrasing does not take the obscenity out of obscene subjects; nor can she imagine anything being lewd that is not openly and affirmatively so."[41]

This, particularly the attack on Ibsen, shows a morbid concern with sexual transgression, one that apparently had a sufficiently powerful emotion behind it to blind him to the main concern of *Hedda Gabler.* Exaggeration of the sexual element also marked his comment on *Crime and Punishment:* "a horribly vulgar and sensational mass of murder and the play of love between a brutal murderer and a scarlet woman."[42]

It is evident from his inclusion of the Pre-Raphaelites among the realists that Thompson's views on the limits of realism were confused by his obsessive identification of realism and sexual misbehavior. Wordsworth and Sainte-Beuve, he believed, "represent pretty fairly the basis of our so-called realistic art; out of them have sprung the Rossettis, the Burne-Joneses, the Zola's and all the lesser folk of the fleshly school." Even Whitman was a realist because he sought to imitate Greek nakedness.[43]

Thompson tried, however, to give his objection to realism a broad philosophical basis. In the most general terms, he opposed it because it was an outgrowth of the materialistic, agnostic, scientific point of view. Realism as a movement he saw as "a period of negative attraction between genius and the prevailing religion." This alienation was not entirely the fault of genius: the rigid literalists in religion refused to assimilate the discoveries of science, and certain recalcitrant geniuses, lacking the sure guidance of religion, tended to misunderstand and misinterpret the moral and philosophical implications of scientific discoveries. This attitude on the part of genius was attributable to what he called the "residual heathenism in our civilization"— a residuum that was being gradually eroded by the steady progress of Christianity. Nevertheless, realism, as it existed for Thompson, was "but another word for materialism and infidelity. If you will scrape off the veneer of realism which scouts at romance, you will find the substance of agnosticism. If you are an agnostic you are a realist; if you are a romancer, you have religion." Thompson thought that Tolstoi's "pretension" of Christianity was probably the most hideous example of this materialistic tendency. "It is worse than any other form of materialism because it professes to believe in Christianity while it clothes the image of Christ in the garments of a mountebank. . . ."[44]

From an esthetic point of view, realism was almost as vicious as from the moral viewpoint, Thompson felt. Because it sprang from scientific-agnostic materialism, it imposed two fatal limitations on itself at the very outset: (1) it accepted science as of universal potency, and (2) it accepted the visible and the tangible as the limits of reality. Therefore, the realist, strictly speaking, is limited to a kind of literary photography. "Someone must pose for him when he wishes to delineate a character in fiction." He may depict only what he has "seen, or touched, or heard, or smelt, or tasted. . . ." Such a literary theory implies, too, an impossible critical theory. For if the artist is a photographer the only question is how well the photograph corresponds to reality, and to judge that the critic must have a detailed knowledge of the milieu being described.[45]

The productions of realism, being limited to photography, can have, said Thompson, only a circumscribed and short-lived appeal. "Realism is essentially of today and for today, whilst the ideal creations of genius are for all time." The realist, in short, has no concern with the eternal values upon which great art must be based. "In this materialistic age everything that cannot be photographed and touched and dissected is rejected as valueless and therefore genius is denied and laughed at."[46] It is this denial of genius that was perhaps his most serious esthetic objection to realism.

According to Thompson, realism vitiates both the fiction and the criticism of those who follow the realists' creed; by the very nature of his assumptions a realist can never be a wise or safe critic. Even Howells, "genial and lovable as he is, cannot hide his contempt for genius; and he is all the time savagely, if indirectly, attacking the methods of Hugo, Scott, Dickens, Goethe and Hawthorne."[47] In the production of fiction, the denial of genius (reliance on Zola's "scientific" method) always leads, Thompson thought, away from vigor, enthusiasm, "imaginative lift," originality, and inventive power—all marks of genius. Sometimes it even seemed to him that those who insisted on the scientific approach did so because they were unable to compass the "artistic" approach. He said, for instance, that the reason Thomas Hardy's stories have unhappy endings is that Hardy's "inventive power is weak, and this, perhaps, has been the chief factor of the force driving him upon realism." Of all the group who scorn genius and heroism Thompson stated:

> The trouble with those who are less than great is their inability to comprehend heroism. Not having the highest order of genius themselves they do not believe that the highest order exists. . . . The man who has felt the wind of battle in his hair; who has heard the glorious wings of death winnowing the smoke of musket and cannon; who has lost himself and found instead his ideal, as he rushed up the currents of bellowing flame and into the mouths of batteries; who has felt the thrilling touch of a comrade on either side and heard the burst of cheers as the hill-top was gained, is ready to pity him who heard but did not respond to the call of the drums of his country; nay ready to forgive him his inability to comprehend that heroism is still a part of manhood. So in art it is only the born genius, the elect climber of Parnassus, who feels the influence of the gods and dares trust himself beyond the limit of the commonplace.[48]

The choice of a military comparison here, if one remembers his early life and his later imperialistic expressions, speaks for itself.

Thompson's other esthetic objections to realism, neither of which he pursued at length, were (1) that it was "art for art's sake" and (2) that it had a completely mercenary basis—it was art for money's sake.[49]

He felt that there were certain social objections, as well, namely, that realism was un-American, a foreign import; that it presented an untrue picture of the society it purported to record; and, by implication, that it was the voice of conservatism, holding America back from the realization of her destiny. As to its foreign origin, "In our country," said Thompson, "the taste for raw and rancid realism is an acquired, not a natural one, however congenial it may be in Russia and France; . . . our Puritan and Huguenot ancestors gave us a strain of moral caution and reserve, a cleanliness, and above all, an hereditament of revolt against social corruption. . . ." If we fail to protect our heritage, thought Thompson, realism will begin to undermine our social forms. The Haymarket Riot seemed to him a primary example of the subversive effect of foreign literature on the American scene; and the executions which followed—the executions which had such a profound effect on Howells and other intellectuals of the time—were for Thompson "a notable event in the history of civilization," an event which marked the beginning of vigorous resistance in America to that foreign treason which was being abetted by European realism.[50]

On the score of misrepresenting American life, Thompson saw the two best-known realists, Howells and James, as illustrative of a general tendency to belittle American culture. It was permissible, he said, for Howells and James to "romance about the crudity of American social culture and literary and artistic attainments, as compared with those of European peoples"; but to present these "romances" as representative of the true situation was dishonest.

H. B. Fuller, along with Howells, was attacked for his portrayal of American urban life. The Cliff-Dwellers and The Rise of Silas Lapham, Thompson believed, "are by no means actual transcripts of life at its fair value in Chicago and Boston. There is a meaning, there is a force in Chicago life not suggested by a light story like 'The Cliff Dwellers'; there is a power, a trend, an exponent of Boston life beside which the humorous vulgarity of 'Silas Lapham' is quite without importance. . . . The assumption that [these books] measure the civilization of those cities is simply preposterous."[51]

When, at the turn of the century, it appeared that romance was winning, both in literature and in life; when the adolescent but nonetheless stirring heroics of Theodore Roosevelt had provided a concrete symbol and rallying point for the imperialist spirit that had been growing rapidly for a decade; and when such literary figures as Garland, Howells, Fuller, and Mark Twain, as members of the Anti-Imperialist League, were opposing the new direction of development because they feared that undemocratic impulses were behind it—then Thompson began to see realism as conservative and therefore undesirable. America was in a season of revolution, he thought, in which "it is new America that is writing as well as living the new romance." The opposition was composed of those "unchangeable conservatives" to whom the old ways always seemed better than the new. They were unable to "feel the freshness of an era blooming at sunrise," but it mattered little because there was nothing they could do to stop the march of Destiny.[52]

Although in his criticism of poetry Thompson always identified with the Ideal poets, in his repeated attempts to characterize Ideal poetry he did not always have clearly in mind what he had said on previous occasions. The result was a congeries of ideas to which the following summary may not do justice. There would seem to be four principal requirements: (1) it must show originality; (2) it must achieve imaginative surprise; (3) it must exert a perennial fascination; and (4) it must be the product of a Seer—that is, it must interpret, prophesy, lead the way for those who are not born to the lyre.

Of originality not much can be said. It is not mere oddity or picturesqueness but rather "a direct, irresistible and before unused appeal to a common and universal sympathy."[53] Thompson was unable to explain it beyond this, and in the examples he cited—Sappho, Theocritus, Villon, Burns, Poe—he did not attempt to specify the precise originality of each. Imaginative surprise is not much clearer. It was for him a certain quality inherent in a poem which causes repeated "surprise" in the reader each time he goes back to the poem; it also seems to be made up of three subspecies of surprise: lyric, dramatic, and descriptive, though these are never analyzed.[54]

The source of "perennial fascination" is variously described. Originality, as set out above, is obviously one source of it, i.e., the universal sympathy of the human soul. Elsewhere Thompson found it in "soul substance." If a lyric is "made of the all-pervading soul-substance it is great," he said. "It grips the hearts of all, high, low, genius, clown, and there is no resisting it."[55] Optimism also is a part of it,[56] as is the poet's heroic attempt at the "expression of inexpressible beauty,"[57] (a phrase which in itself has a certain fascination!). The passion of love, which he regarded as a major source of art, is another part of Ideal poetry. He made both an essay and a poem of the Pan-Syrinx fable, but he quickly extended the application of his thwarted-desire theory beyond physical love to the realm of unrealized aspiration in general. Still he warned that it is just as wrong to conceive of poetry as wholly spiritual in origin as to call it wholly physical. Moreover, "love and war touch elbows as they walk. . . . To love and to fight are the two deepest set and most firmly imbedded elementary instincts of the manly nature." Hence the perennial fascination of love songs and war songs.[58] Finally, "purity of vision," a quality which Thompson ascribed to Gilder's work, he also found perennially fascinating.[59]

The fourth quality of Ideal poetry is its prophetic, interpretive character, which, in turn, seems to be divided into two main areas: the interpretations of God's meanings, the expression of eternal truth; and the expression of the culture and the aspirations of the time and place in which the Ideal poet lives. The first must be expressed "in unison with" the second.[60]

A problem which plagued the defenders of Ideality in the post-Civil War era was the growing popularity of poets unorthodox in their metrics: Emerson, Emily Dickinson, Browning, and Whitman preeminently. To Thompson the question took the form of a choice between the esthetic appeal of refinement and the undeniably rude power of the broken rhythms, irregular patterns, and imperfect rhymes. At one time he could go so far as to say that there was a "huge truth . . . in the form of a law which withdraws strength in proportion to the increment of technical refinement."[61] He could also say that "Whitman is tolerated, even encouraged, in resentment of a plethora of placid smoothness with which our rhythmic literature is flooded"; and although he could not respect Whitman as a poet, he did respect him "as a man with the genius to feel the need of a revolution in style."[62] He admitted that Emily Dickinson's poems "seem to gain a certain power from halting rhythms and incomplete rhymes,"[63] and that in all his reading he had never found a more interesting book of verse, "one with so

many beauties almost buried in so many blemishes."[64] Browning
and Emerson he admired together, for he felt that they were marked
by the same virtues and the same shortcomings. "Surcharged with
song, but . . . with vocal organs not of the singing sort, . . . they
forgot the tune in the tremendous struggle with the meaning of
the words, and they lost the words too often in the overwhelming
rush of thought."[65]

When Thompson spoke of the more orthodox poets of his own
day or the acknowledged masters of earlier times, he was able to
command more confidence and to praise without reservation. Stedman, Aldrich, Gilder, and Poe were "true singers." "The Raven,"
he said, stands as "a lonely and incomparably beautiful landmark
in the history of American imaginative verse. We but belittle our
best when we belittle it . . . . Nothing in the poetry of Emerson,
Longfellow, Lowell or Bryant, comes near it in absolute originality
of conception, in the fitting of musical diction to a human mood,
or in wealth of unhackneyed imaging."[66] This dictum, when added
to further opinions that blank verse is the "highest and noblest"
form of poetic expression and that if Gilder had made his poems
three hundred years ago "we might now be writing long apprecia-
tions of [them],"[67] placed Thompson pretty clearly on the side of
orthodoxy in form.

Another indication of his conservatism and gentility was his
unflagging opposition to dialect verse. Although he knew James
Whitcomb Riley as a personal friend, he was never willing to
praise Riley's work except as a bit of "delightful fooling for an
evening's entertainment." And he always believed that Riley's
real appeal came not from his use of dialect but from his striking
the chords of a "universal human sympathy," a feat which might
be more lastingly and tellingly achieved within the bounds of the
refined poetic tradition. "Will 'Eyes like two fried aigs, / And a
nose like a Bartlett pear' ripen," he asked, "as wine ripens, down
the years?"[68]

Although he never expressed any great admiration for Sidney
Lanier, he was affected by that poet's emphasis on the musical
quality of verse. He believed that the music and color (defined as
the result of "using the pen like a brush") of verse are appealing
and enjoyable entirely apart from the meaning; but he was always
careful to distinguish between "word power" and "thought power,"
emphasizing that both are important to great poetry. To Thomp-

son, Lanier's concentration on word power to the neglect of the other was his weakness.[69]

As for future developments in poetic form, Thompson looked, paradoxically, to Emerson to lead the way. He believed that poetry would become more concerned with thought than with phrase and that Emerson, "with his rough, loaded verses," pointed in the new direction. Implicit in this judgment is a distinction, not evident in the other essays, between "thought power" and didacticism. It was not elaborated in this context, but it was a valid perception on Thompson's part.

In all of Thompson's writing about poetry there is a tendency to limit discussion to the lyric. Without saying categorically that lyric poetry is the only true poetry, he tends to ignore other types. And he does say that the lyric is the *highest* form of poetry because it is the expression of great personality; and the expression of great personality is the mark of genius.[70] Although he was a great admirer of Stedman, he had no interest at all in Stedman's theory that dramatic poetry was due for a revival in America. And although he dutifully included Shakespeare every time he made a list of "geniuses," there is nothing in his writings to indicate that his interest was anything more than dutiful, and there is at least one essay which suggests that his interest in, his comprehension of, and his appreciation for Shakespeare were slight.[71] When he deigned to discuss dramatic poetry as such, it was only to try to prove that there is no real difference between the dramatic and lyric modes.[72] Narrative poetry also received little attention, unless it included a strong lyric element. Chaucer was not a poet—just a good storyteller who put his stories into rhyme.[73] And although Thompson again dutifully included Homer among the geniuses, it was Theocritus and Sappho who received his endless praise and loving attention. Finally there was his repeated assertion that Keats's "Ode to a Nightingale"— a poem preeminently lyric—is the greatest poem in the English language.

Thompson's criticism of poetry was not the major part of his work, for in addition to his concern with realism in fiction, he was greatly interested in the circumstances of literary production in postbellum America, the character of the literary market, and the situation of the writer.

One of his most persistent objections was to the force of eastern and urban tastes in determining what should be published, both in books and in magazines, and what should be approved once it was published. This opposition to urban taste was not apparent in Thompson's early work. In 1878 he was still of the opinion that "literature, no matter how desirable or how much desired, can never originate or thrive, to any satisfactory extent, outside the great cities. . . ."[74] But his objections began to develop during the 1880's, when he was struggling to establish himself as a writer, and when he, along with a great many midwesterners, began to feel that theirs was a homegrown culture in which they could take pride; and he returned to the theme frequently to the end of his life. Of course his strictures were not without a note of personal pique, but they have a much larger significance as expressions of the situation confronting residents of the "Hoosier Athens" as well as of the whole aspiring Midwest.

The basic accusation was that eastern editors and critics and writers were ignorant of the true America. Less than a score of men, he said in 1891, "control in a large degree, not only the quantity, but also the quality of fictitious literature produced in America. And these controlling men are not representative Americans; they are representative of merely the literary taste of one or two cities where taste has been filed down and sand-papered to conventional dimensions."[75] The result was that urban editors fostered an untrue picture of American culture, chiefly through their insistence that western and southern and New England writers give them realistic dialect "yawp" and local color. (Here it might be well to recall Garland's statement that "there was a cult of the vernacular in 1888 and Gilder was its high priest.")[76] But to Thompson's mind such literature did violence to the "push" and idealism of American life. The entire output of the New England school could be boiled down, as far as he was concerned, to "one story of a New England spinster whose lover was a widower, and the story of a Boston girl who mastered a fad, lived an old maid, and died unhappy." And of Indiana's own poet he said, "Riley's Hoosierland is in fact as much an abstraction as Faerieland, or Avalon, or Hesperides." Fully as important as the injustice to American civilization was the injustice and positive harm that urban editors were doing to writers by forcing them constantly "to saw on one string." George Washington Cable was limited to New Orleans, Mary Noailles Murfree to Tennessee, Joel Chandler Harris and Richard M. Johnston to Georgia. Such specialism, said Thompson, stultifies genius and "dwarfs the artist's creations."[77]

The editors also fostered sectional feeling in life and literature through their cultivation of local color and dialect, Thompson felt. Although at one time he was inclined to justify sectionalism in literature as a *de facto* condition, and even a virtue, he later came to regard it as unpatriotic and unsuitable to prevailing conditions. Writing in 1884 he said that "New England and the South are two unalterable and clearly limited sections," and that out of these regions "must come the material for the truly American fiction and poetry," because the West is culturally amorphous. "It begins nowhere and ends nowhere and can never be typified in literature or art any more than it can be geographically limited." Two years later he accused Gilder of a "narrow Eastern mood—a N.Y. mood" in his editing of the *Century*. And in 1892 he took a view almost opposite from his first stand, a view in keeping with the myth of the cultural homogeneity of the Anglo-Saxon, when he said, "I cannot see why there should be any Southern writers, any New England writers, any Western writers, or any localized writers of any kind in this country. We are American; our writers, all who are worth having, are American writers, and as Americans they write for the world."[78]

This insistence on the national character of American literature was part of a larger protest against the tendency of eastern critics and publishers, probably aided by the magazine editors, to indulge in a specious kind of "cosmopolitanism," with the result that good American books were slighted while inferior foreign books were "boomed." Thompson saw the situation as growing out of two factors: the intellectual subservience of American to European critics and the lack of international copyright. The first was no new thing, he thought: "Many years ago that acute but ill-tempered critic, Edgar Poe, called attention to our kiss-me-mamma attitude toward England in everything pertaining to our growth in letters."[79]

As to the pretense of cosmopolitanism, nothing could be further from a basis in true art; a universal, supernational world literature would, in Thompson's view, be no literature at all. He even went so far as to say that "every impulse toward universality in art is self-conscious and artificial, a process of grafting and cross-fertilization that dissipates originality and abolishes all the sharp outlines of nativity." Remembering that he was a defender of the Good, the True, and the Beautiful, he qualified this statement by saying that in addition to the individual, national appeal there is also a universal appeal in great art, but he still insisted that "the chief barrier to American art is the lack of Americanism in the broadest and deepest sense."[80]

For international copyright Thompson argued long and loud, the gist of his contention being that the situation without copyright was morally disgraceful as well as artistically and politically dangerous. "Our book-stores are but whitened literary fence-dens," he said: the Congressional attitude amounted to the encouragement of theft, theft not only from foreigners but also, in effect, from American authors, who were forced to work for starvation wages by the publishers' free access to foreign books. This had a double effect on art: on the one hand it retarded the development of American art by killing off American artists, so to speak; on the other it generated an untrue and unpatriotic art, for "the fiction that we read shapes in some degree the fiction that we write." And since Thompson was also convinced that the fiction one reads shapes moral and social ideals, the flood of foreign fiction was for him a kind of creeping poison; it represented a clear, if not a present danger: "An alien art brings with it a touch of the foreign soil. . . . The civilization of Great Britain is the opposite of a republican civilization; that of France is even more pronounced in its attitude of antagonism to that crystal purity of democratic patriotism upon which, if anything, must forever depend the perpetuity of our national life. The political nihilism and the social gloom and pessimism of Russian fiction are said to be fairly representative of the trend of Russian national influence."[81]

Thompson saw the publishers' greed for profits as a moral force (which it certainly was) rather than as an economic force (which it certainly was also), and he regarded the passage of the copyright law in 1891 as a moral victory brought about by moral forces. These are facts which underline the predominantly ethical temper of his mind. If later and better-informed commentators have seen the passage of the law as mainly the result of the publishers' own recognition that the uncertain status of literary property was leading to cutthroat and ruinous competition,[82] Thompson's moral fervor is more representative of contemporary attitudes.

To Thompson, there was something about city life that was deadly to literature because it was deadly to morals. Generally speaking, his indictment depended more on rhetoric than on details—he said, for instance, that when a literary man goes off to New York he is sure "to be swallowed up in Trade, Tammany, and Turmoil"—but there is sufficient specific comment to show that one of his principal objections was to the sexual misbehavior which he felt the anonymity of city life encouraged. "The debaucheries of city life" generate in the urban critic and urban writer a taste for a specious "virility," which he identified with "unholy love" in all its forms from flirtation to adultery.

Another objection was that city life was conventional and artificial, that it had no basis in the unchanging realities of life. The provincial's vision "goes back to the blue hills of Pindar, and the well-head of Ecclesiastes. [The urbanite's] flattens against the billboards of Ibsen. The street is contemporary; the country is now and always and ever, the past, the present and the endless future, spiritually unchangeable."[83] More specifically, the urbanite was ignorant of nature, a prepotent factor for both the artist and the critic.

As antidotes to these narrow eastern and urban moods, Thompson stood solidly in favor of the western and the provincial. The isolation that once marked provincial life was a thing of the past since the advent of railroads, the telegraph, and rapid distribution of printed matter. Republican institutions, too, had "equalized life" to such a degree that the provincial was "in perfect rapport with the most advanced metropolitan spirit." As evidence of the advanced spirit of the West, Thompson cited the Western Association of Writers, founded at Indianapolis in 1886, the federation of ladies' literary clubs in Indiana, by which "the enlightenment of literature enters our homes through the purest channels," and finally "Wabash College where. . .our youths dwell for six years in much the same atmosphere as that of Oxford or Cambridge—a bit fresher perhaps, and purer. . . ." He was also a great advocate of Chicago's possibilities as a literary center, feeling, evidently, that the midwestern atmosphere would keep Chicago litterateurs cleansed of urban sins. The Columbian Exposition of 1893, he believed, afforded an excellent opportunity for launching a literary magazine that might shift the center of American culture from New York, just as the founding of Scribner's and Harper's had shifted it from Boston. Chicago, he said, was sure to be the western reservoir of energy in literature and art. "In the next ten years Chicago must and will respond to the demand of the millions of reading people who already look to her gates for their supplies of everything save literature."[84] Though Thompson never said so specifically, he probably felt that the promise of the Columbian Exposition was not fulfilled. *The Chap-Book*, founded in 1894, though in the main genteel, was not adamantly so and had faded away by 1898; and the growing power of the "Chicago Gang" was often antagonistic to the literary ideals that Thompson espoused. Therefore it is not surprising to find him turning at the end of his life to booming Indiana as a cultural center. According to Lew Wallace, Thompson was one of a group "working ever so deftly and successfully to lift Indiana out of the depths, and set her high up in the world of literature." Although Thompson's preference for Indiana was implict in his defense of the West—the evidence he adduced was mostly drawn from the Indiana scene—the evidence of the campaign which Wallace mentioned did not appear until the last summer of Thompson's life. In a relatively long essay in the *Independent* he wrote a heated protest against the invidious connotation attached to the term "Hoosier" and a defense of the cultural adequacy, if not supremacy, of Indiana.[85]

Literature as business often occupied Thompson's thoughts and his pen. He was repelled by the money-grabbing aspects of American life; but since laissez faire and "push" were part of a larger cultural pattern which he revered, in most instances he stood up for them in spite of his revulsion. To a sympathetic spirit like Howells (this was the year that Howells had visited Crawfordsville) he confessed that "there is something inexorable in business affairs which has often hit me pretty hard." But to Gilder he presented a sturdy and orthodox front. He said bluntly that he thought his work was worth more than the rate Gilder paid but added, "You must not understand me as grumbling. I look upon the sordid part of this thing as 'business,' of course, and the *Century* has the right to make its own terms. I'm no striker."[86] And in a good part of his public utterances on the subject, this same facet of his personality was apparent. He subscribed fully to the principle of laissez faire in the literary market. He wanted the cash-sale method. The author, he believed, was like any other man who sells his labor: he is entitled to a wage rather than a lottery ticket for his work. He also expected the literary man to get for his products everything the market would bear, and once he roundly denounced Andrew Lang for saying that an editor paid him too much for a poem: "A pump-maker would have better judgment," said Thompson. In his presidential address to the second annual meeting of the Western Association of Writers he assured the aspiring provincials (some of whom, he knew, were pitifully lacking in talent) that the literary market differed in no wise from the wheat market. "Supply and demand rule. . . Competition keeps the market healthy." From time to time, however, he felt that there was too much competition. Like the eastern author at an Indiana lyceum who thoughtlessly invited all authors in the audience to sit on the platform with him, only to see the audience rise as one man and head for the stage, Thompson was almost overwhelmed by the throng of hopeful scribblers trying to get into print. The supply so far exceeded the demand that those afflicted with *cacoethes scribendi* succeeded only in starving the whole race of authors, themselves included.[87] But this situation only reinforced his conclusion that in literature, business is business. The implication of such a view of the literary market is that the test of value in art is popular taste, the taste of the buying public. It is an implication that troubled Thompson, for as necessary as it was to his viewpoint, he could not wholly accept it, as we have seen.

Thompson's criticism of society is marked by a vague and insistent optimism mixed with moments of uncertainty and despair. But it is mostly the optimism that received conscious expression. He hoped, for instance, for a sectless Christianity, a gradual healing of the "persistent, refractory wounds on the fair body of religion," for a day when the "cord of creed drawn overtight" no longer threatened to "strangle what it was noosed to save," when a homogeneous Christianity should be able to "set its ethical standard on the temple of life, and the temple of art."[88]

He also defended, sometimes fearfully, sometimes expansively, the forms and values of the Protestant middle-class society which dominated American culture in his day. Clearly he stood in the tradition of E. L. Godkin and the conservative, moral reformers whose desire it was to put down the abuses and purify the system of laissez-faire capitalism. Wealth, property, and laissez faire were Christian institutions according to Thompson; they were ordained by a "natural law given to all life by God" and were in no way affected by the teachings of Christ relative to the salvation of the soul: "I do not believe that wealth is inimical to Christianity. On the contrary, I think Christianity brings wealth and prosperity to the peoples who embrace it. History shows that the evolution of Christianity has been along the line of lawfully gained and wisely protected wealth.[89] Edward Bellamy's Nationalist movement, he believed, pandered "to the lowest sort of envy, jealousy, and prejudice harbored by the unsuccessful and soured side of society against the successful and happy side of it." The worst service to be done society, the worst service to be done the poor, for that matter, was to set one class against the other.[90] Accordingly, Thompson opposed the organization of labor, but for another reason, too—organization meant an abridgment of the laborer's God-given freedom. All free men are laborers, he thought, and only laborers are free men; and "so soon as [the laborer] ceases to be a laborer he is no longer free, and so the danger to organized laborers bound in a body is the loss of personal liberty in the loss of the right to labor at will."[91] But he was not entirely blind to the problems which labor faced in his day. Behind his complaint to Gilder about low rates of pay there lay a vague realization that his own situation was that of a laborer whose pay was not commensurate with the work he did because he was at the mercy of an editor who could draw on a free labor market. Still, his ingrained middle-class bias kept him from identifying himself with the laboring classes—pushed him, in fact, into siding with those who were grinding him down. Howells saw the problem much more clearly than Thompson ever did when he said, "Perhaps [the author] will never be at home anywhere in the world as long as there are masses whom he ought to consort with, and classes whom he cannot consort with."[92]

But Thompson's most violent attack was against the "Tolstoian heresy leading to anarchy or communism." Tolstoi he abused as a "worn-out *roué*—a satiated and engorged criminal—a jaundiced, filth-soaked carcass of sin and shame—the rotten hull of a man whose youth and prime are gone, spent in hideous excesses, who would now turn in his old days when lust is exhausted, and set the world the true pattern of Christ."[93] Still Thompson was more consistent than some of his contemporaries in defending wealth as a Christian goal. He believed that it was time to purge the pulpit of that nonsense about money being the root of all evil and the poor being the truly blessed.[94] He did not go so far as to recommend expurgating the Bible.

As one might expect, he also defended social status—not as a corollary of economic status but as a *de facto* situation having its basis in human nature, as witnessed by the fact that the whole world gives tacit approval: "We understand, but never breathe it aloud, that riding the high-horse is a little game at which we are all playing for all there is in it."[95]

But behind his confident defense of bourgeois society lurked a fear about the future that he occasionally expressed. His aversion to Bellamy's Nationalism was a mild example of it, as was his break with the Democratic party over Populism and Free Silver. In men like Ignatius Donnelly, General James B. Weaver, and "Sockless Jerry" Simpson (the epithet alone would have been enough to repel Thompson) he saw a real threat to the stability of society. Another example was his moment of rhetorical despair in the late 1880's when realism seemed to be gaining ground: "The revolution now threatening our country is in its early stage. The progression will be: Realism, sensualism, materialism, socialism, communism, nihilism, absolute anarchy. Each of these is a form of death." Even at the end of the century the victory of William McKinley and romance might be only temporary: "Life is worth living in our day, but after us how will it be? A moment's reflection satisfies me that I am near deep water. . . ."[96] So great was Thompson's fear of anarchy that he implicitly denied the Lockean right of revolution against intolerable government. It might well be, he said, that Russian laws were bad and the Russian government oppressive, but any law is better than anarchy. He did not say what the recourse from intolerable laws should be.[97]

But in spite of his fears Thompson was often sanguine about America's future, if for no other reason than the great resilience of character in the "genuine American"—"a plausible, querulous, aggressive, enterprising, crafty fellow, who tries every mode of getting a livelihood, and always with success." It was this type of person who had spread over the West, who in Indiana had "made a paradise out of an ague-plagued wilderness within the thirty years last past," and who might be expected to prevail in the future.[98] The only threat to this Arcadian picture of western farm life that Thompson saw was the encroachment of technology: the threshing machine's "cruel teeth" at the intake might mangle an arm, and the speed of the machine imposed an inhuman strain on the laborer who must keep up with it. He had seen men, he said, "come forth from that storm of chaff, straw, dust, and what not of stifling vegetable compound, looking more dead than alive, panting for breath, bathed in sweat and trembling from over-exertion."[99] He was, however, comforted by a belief that the limits of science and technology had been reached, for all working purposes, and that America was "entering the larger atmosphere of conscious intellectual life," in which democracy would be the informing spirit of a new literature, a new politics, a new educational system.[100]

The Chicago Columbian Exposition was the occasion for a less nebulous kind of optimism. When Thompson, along with E. C. Stedman, Horace Scudder, Charles Dudley Warner, Washington Gladden, Agnes Repplier, and others, was invited by the editors of the *Critic* to give his impressions of the fair, he replied in a characteristic vein—characteristic of a waxing American imperialism as well as of his own militaristic and chauvinistic tendencies. He was overwhelmed by the greatness, goodness, energy, and intelligence of the American people: "My country's life pulsating around me, the heart throb of modern Rome—America the young, the strong, the master of destiny, the unarmed and open-breasted conqueror of the world."[101] These sentiments forecast perfectly the jingoism which later marked his poetry and fiction.

For the future, Thompson's one specific object of fear was the Negro. In a pair of essays for the *Independent* he tried to rationalize this fear in scientific terms by stating a "law of nature" which requires every human, black or white, to pass on his color undefiled to his offspring and by adducing evidence to show the dire results of mixing. Thompson saw two possible courses of action: legal, rigidly enforced segregation or the annihilation of one race by the other, according to the law of survival of the fittest.[102] That he should regard these as the only alternatives indicates both his uncompromising and absolutistic turn of mind and his sensitivity to the currents of Darwinian thought in the period.

In connection with the Negro problem, Thompson also wrote a not entirely covert defense of lynching. Although he purported to be objectively reporting facts and attitudes about lynching in the United States, his own attitudes clearly emerge. (He often said of himself, "I cannot simulate.") His argument was that the English and American judicial tradition of assuming the accused innocent until proven guilty may be the luxury of an outworn age: "That may be an archaic maxim of the law books, assuming an ethical preference for coddling many criminals rather than injuring one innocent suspect. The larger truth, however, is that society and civilization are built upon the sacrificial bones of harmless individuals necessarily offered up for the good of the many. . . . In the long run it is the certainty of fate that counts. Inevitable death for the crime of rape is what Southern popular feeling demands."[103]

As a critic Thompson was a curious mixture of admirable and not-so-admirable qualities. He showed courage, passionate sincerity, enthusiasm, and, above all, a sense of dedication. He had a profound conviction of his obligation to do everything in his power to foster the spread of the best life that he knew. And this he did. At the same time he inclined toward a sometimes incredible misstatement of his opponents' positions, an arrogant dogmatism, and even personal abuse. It should thus be clear that his manner was fully as important as his matter in any estimate of his criticism.

His religious and social heritage and the Crawfordsville milieu into which he fitted this heritage help to explain some of his characteristics. The zealous and evangelical tone of his criticism may have come from his consciousness that he was descended of preachers who had helped to make the West the thriving and respectable region that he knew and loved. For this conclusion there is more evidence than just similarity of tone and method: he devoted an entire essay to eulogizing the role that the Baptist preachers played in western settlement, to the "great work" they did in fighting "evil in dark, isolated places," and to their "downright honesty [which] forbade diplomatic evasions" (an indirect defense of his own method in criticism). The religious heritage also helps to explain his feeling that, in a small way, he was both messiah and martyr. In his later years he said, "Probably there was never a critical truth which was popular in the day of its utterance. . . . The master critic, however, is born to his work, and must suffer for it. . . . High vantage ground proves a lonely abiding spot in the days when nobody cares for what is high. . . ."[104] And of course his religious heritage was an obvious source for the ethical set of his mind and for his deep sense of human nature's frailty, as it is also for the sin-sex identification that injected an almost frantic emotional element into his criticism and contributed to some gross misinterpretations of writers such as Tolstoi and Dostoievsky. His version of *Crime and Punishment* has already been cited. Another typical instance is his almost incredible twisting of Tolstoi's nonresistance to evil: "Tolstoi and all the evil storytellers hold that it is not only useless but wrong to resist evil desire, evil passion, evil temptation; for if it is wrong to resist one evil it is wrong to resist any other."[105]

His economic and social ideals and ambitions, which played a part in his defense of plutocratic forces (he would have opposed them had he recognized them as such), must have been influenced by both his early life and his Crawfordsville life. The ideal of social gentility evident throughout his work clearly owed much to the glimpses he had and the traditions he cherished of upper-class life in the antebellum South. His coming from a class in the South which was halfway up the social ladder would, if the psychology of emulation be true, strengthen his commitment to the social values of the class above him. At the same time, the nineteenth-century Protestant values of thrift and industry must have been held in high regard by a minister's family. Thus Thompson was also in a position to appreciate the values of the midwestern bourgeois society from which his family originally came and into which he married. And since he was more or less insulated by the Indiana milieu from a realization of the effects that were being wrought on American society by a growing plutocracy's completely amoral application of laissez faire, it was almost inevitable that he should support the ideals which, so far as he could see, had generated the society which he enjoyed and respected and wished to preserve for his children. He was not completely ignorant of the fact that amorality existed in the business world and that it posed a threat to the social ideals he espoused.[106] But like a great many high-minded men of his time, he had faith in the potency of ethical and moral forces to keep the recalcitrant elements of the business community in line—a faith that was not justified by the events which followed and was therefore derided by many intellectuals of the 1920's and 1930's.

The tendency toward racism and imperialism was probably rooted in Thompson's Revolutionary heritage and in both southern and midwestern influences. As Merle Curti points out, the idea of white supremacy was solidified even in Colonial times by the rationalization of the settlers' attitude that Indians were "varmints." The slave-master relationship of the antebellum era was an influence in the same direction. Both factors contributed to the white man's belief in his reforming mission.[107] Thus it is no accident that two of the best-known voices of imperialism—the Reverend Josiah Strong and Senator Albert Beveridge—were midwesterners, closer in both time and space to the Indian and the Negro than were residents of the East and North. And thus it is that Thompson's less-known voice is raised in the same cry.

Certain other personal factors are less easy to account for: his dogmatic and judicial temper, for instance. Skepticism and uncertainty, lack of authority, were intellectually intolerable for him. "Montaigne was not a philosopher," he said, "for suspended judgment is not philosophy; no more is mere impartial skepticism."[108] This conclusion might result from the authoritarian habits of mind that go along with fundamentalism in religion, but it might also result from intangible psychological factors such as emotional insecurity. The frequent self-contradictions in Thompson's writing point toward a basic instability in his personality.

Sometimes his dogmatism served to disguise an irresponsible ignorance of literary history. A case in point was his assertion that it was the "spirit of Avon" in Shakespeare's work which made him popular with Londoners and that if Shakespeare were then alive urban editors would delete all that was appealing in his work or would dismiss him if he refused to conform to urban tastes. Another instance was the genealogy of romance and realism which he gave, as required reading, to students of the Chautauqua "graduate course in literature." Romance, he said, descended from the Greek tragedians, through Chaucer, Shakespeare, and Scott; realism descended from the effeminacies of Lyly's *Euphues*. "In [Lyly's] style, bad as it was, can be felt the crude elements of the present analytical method which is the distinctive feature of current realism." Nor was his ignorance confined to minute details remote in time and place. Of Hawthorne he said that his writing showed no formative period, that "he was full-grown at the start"—a statement that must come as a shock to anyone who has made more than a cursory comparison of *Fanshawe* and *The Scarlet Letter*— and that if Hawthorne were influenced by anyone, it was by Poe, an influence that would be chronologically impossible if the first statement about Hawthorne were true.[109]

An unusual sensitivity to the opinions of others is also evident in Thompson's writings, in spite of various explicit statements to the contrary. Like all humans, he thrived on praise, but it was more necessary to him than to most. And, conversely, opposition or disapproval was likely to have a stronger effect on him. To Howells he wrote, "One of the chief fascinations of writing is anticipating and realizing the sympathetic appreciation accorded by one's friends"; or to R. U. Johnson of the *Century*. "I'm not a bit too old to be flattered into spasms." The other side of the picture is evident in the crushing effect which Gilder's refusal of the biographical sketch had on him. Possible reflexes of this sensitivity were his need to win, at almost any cost up to and including personal abuse, and his tendency to justify to a tiresome extent his views and methods. The need to win may also have been a contributing factor in his frequent misinterpretations of his opponents' positions; he even misquoted Riley as the basis for one attack, and when his error was pointed out to him he was genuinely contrite and bewildered at how he repeatedly misread the lines in question and even erroneously transcribed them into his review. His tendency to become snarled in contradictory implications may also have been involved here—that is, his overweening desire to win led him to attack realism on many different, and sometimes contradictory, grounds.[110]

The hatchet-swinging that has been evident in much of his criticism did not pass without sharp comments from other critics and editors, although Howells, one of his most frequent targets, never deigned to answer him by name. But each comment from those who did answer him directly set him anew to defending his method. He cited Poe's example as one means of justifying himself: he "said harsh things, was indeed a bit of a blackguard; [but] he was a true critic, scorning to make friends by the demagog's equivocal phrasing." But his main defense was that perfect sincerity demands unadorned statement; understatement, wit, lightness of touch he had no use for; to his way of thinking, "Ye cayn't kill er rattlesnake too dead." It was only "careless thinkers" who were apt to confuse "perfect sincerity" with offensiveness.[111] These statements are, of course, his conscious explanations of why he wrote as he did.

One other pervasive quality of Thompson's critical writing is stylistic—a kind of fatal glibness. The words appear to have come so easily that even he was taken in by the sound. Sometimes it took the form of specious analogy, of which the following is a good example: "If in writing a book we must not steal the thought-work of a fellow, surely in the same pages we must avoid breaking the other nine commandments." By the use of "in the same pages" he put what goes on in the story into the same category as what goes on in the process of writing the story, thus equating a real crime with an imaginative account of crime. At other times it might be called equivocation, as in this sentence, which was intended to show the connection between art and ethics: "If ethics broadly stated is the art of conduct, in our present discussion we shall find it to be conduct of art."[112] His fondness for clichés is another aspect of this glibness—one of his favorites was the distinction between freedom and license. Although clichés offend the critical reader, they probably were accepted by most of Thompson's readers as old and comfortable friends, easing and speeding communication. Less easy to explain, and impossible to document, is an unspecific quality of glibness. Thompson had the ability to establish and maintain a flow of words which, by the volume and velocity of the stream, so to speak, keeps the reader off balance. It is a strange and insistent loquacity, and it would appear to be a factor in generating what influence Thompson had with the editors and the public of his day.

There are two other factors, however, that would seem to be even more important. The first is that Thompson's taste was wonderfully congenial to a large segment of both the reading and the writing public. His opinions were the opinions that were current, probably in more discreet diction; among Chautauqua circles, ladies' and gentlemen's literary societies, and minor respectable writers (who comprise the greater part of the writing public at any given moment). As James Lane Allen remarked in 1886, "The man who cannot criticize Howells nowadays isn't respectable."[113] And the *Independent,* which represented remarkably well the opinions of the liberal Protestant clergy and the middle class, reflected strong support for Thompson's position during the 1890's from such writers as Edgar Fawcett, Margaret Deland, Agnes Repplier, Kate Upson Clark, Higginson, Warner, and Stoddard. There were a few essays by Tolstoi and some in defense of Howellsian realism by H. H. Boyesen, but the weight was plainly on the side of genteel conservatism.

Second, Thompson's bumptiousness and abusiveness and the controversies he got into as a result of these qualities put him very much in the public eye. It may have been for this reason that the editor of the *Independent,* announcing Thompson's appointment to the staff, felt warranted in commenting, "He has risen fast. . . ." That he did rise quickly perhaps proves again that any publicity is good publicity, for some of his was strong censure, particularly in Boston where his vituperations against Howells and Tolstoi were resented. Thompson's attack on them in his address to the Western Association of Writers in June, 1887, touched off an exchange in· the *Literary World* which, viewed from this distance, puts Thompson in a very bad light; but doubtless it generated for him support·and approval among his contemporaries. His part in the controversy consisted simply in repeating, in letters to the *Literary World* and in an article for the Chicago *Sunday Times,* his accusations that Tolstoi was a crank, a brutal vulgarian, a "heartless theorist who sends his daughters out to work in the field with peasants," a man of filthy and debauched appetites who dressed like a clown and pretended to be a shoemaker in order to attract attention, and that because he was all those things Howells had fallen in love with him and impugned the motives of anyone who attacked his idol. The editors finally had to break off the argument because it became clear that Thompson was not going to break it off, and successive letters added nothing new to the substance of his indictment. But the editors ended with a warning that, compared to Thompson's part in the argument, was very temperate:

> We take it upon ourselves to warn the readers of the Chicago *Sunday Times,* so far as we can reach them, and so far as they have read Mr. Thompson and not read Mr. Howells, that his representations of Mr. Howells, as of Tolstoi, are misrepresentations, and that they do Mr. Howells a grievous wrong. And to Mr. Thompson we beg leave to suggest that truthfulness is the first weapon of the critic, and until he has learned the art of stating the case with which he is dealing in fair terms he would better leave it alone. It is no honor to American letters that a reputable and sincere author can be spoken of in the public press in a way at once so inaccurate, so intemperate, and so abusive.[114]

Only a little less sharp, but logically more telling, was Thompson's exchange with George Trumbull Ladd, a Yale professor who was a pioneer in American experimental psychology. The details are too lengthy to go into; it is enough to note that Ladd very neatly rebuked him for his penchant for personalities and also seriously questioned, from the point of view of experimental psychology, his assumptions about the moral effect of art. Thompson did not answer Ladd's last contribution.[115]

Thompson also entered into a heated but inconclusive exchange with John Burroughs over Whitman's alleged indecency.[116] He became involved with Edmund Gosse and Andrew Lang when he atacked the insularity of English critics because they had no appreciation of western literature. Even Joseph and Jeanette Gilder, who were generally in sympathy with his attitudes, occasionally took him to task for his quixotic manner—especially when he nipped at eastern editors.

It was these factors that made him welcome to the *Independent* and to *America*. The editors of *The Chap-Book* also used him to reinforce the "respectability" of that journal after H. T. Peck's *Bookman* published some aspersions on its morality because its editorial policy seemed a little too tolerant of Howells, Zola, Garland, and Tolstoi.[117]

Other of Thompson's contemporaries valued him for much the same reason as the editors of the *Independent,* that is, for his fearless, often slashing attacks on realism and anything else suggestive of moral or literary conventions unfriendly to those which respectable middle-class society had learned to revere. Stedman, for example, wrote to him in 1899, "You have said many stout and sane things, which I often have felt it on my American conscience to try to say myself." And Paul Elmer More, who succeeded him as literary editor of the *Independent,* recalled that Thompson "was a man of decided tastes and had made a brave fight . . . for what is sound and strong in literature."[118]

Yet Thompson's interest, and the interests of his social group, went far beyond the preservation of economic security, as the bourgeois morality has often been explained. Their culture was, in a narrow sense, a Christian humanism, based on a genuine conviction that the life of the spirit, the eternal life of the soul, was important and was to be achieved through rigid adherence to the Ten Commandments, and that at the same time life on this earth was a valuable experience in itself, which, by the same commandments, could be made more beautiful and more comfortable than it was. Such other virtues as courtesy, bravery, and reverence for women were respected not only because they were economically useful but also because they were morally beautiful. Artistic and intellectual achievements were revered not wholly because they represented conspicuous leisure but because they were intellectually and spiritually satisfying as well.

If that culture, as a Christian culture, exhibited ideas about wealth that may seem hard to reconcile with Christ's teachings and if it also developed in places such ugly excrescences as racism and imperialism, conceiving them as progressive and Christian attitudes, who can say that its vision of beauty was thereby wholly invalidated? And, if economic forces which that culture did not recognize proved more potent in shaping the America of the twentieth century than the moral forces which it did recognize, who can say that the believers deserve only scorn for their faith?

For all these reasons, and more, Thompson as a critic is a confused and confusing figure. Strongly motivated by this vision of spiritual life, moral beauty, and social grace, and passionately dedicated to its defense, he was too passionately dedicated to proceed on his mission with equanimity. Thus, he used methods which can hardly be called admirable even in the light of the values he was defending. Had the issues mattered less to him, perhaps we might now be able to read him with greater sympathy.

CHAPTER IV

THE POET

IF THOMPSON'S FRIENDS during his mature years thought of him mainly as a nature writer and if the public knew him best as a critic, some commentators have been no less inclined to believe him mainly a poet. When the editor of *Scott's* announced in January, 1869, that the next issue would carry the first installment of a new serial "written by J. Maurice Thompson, the eccentric poet, novelist and reviewer,"[1] he implied in the same paragraph that his readers were already familiar with the work of this "brilliant and successful literateur [*sic*]," especially in the field of poetry. In the same year James Wood Davidson, in his highly inclusive study of southern writers, gave Thompson a relatively long treatment, declaring that "it is as a poet that Mr. Thompson has taken most distinctive position."[2] Sixty-five years later Frank H. Ristine felt that "it is on the poems that his most enduring fame will probably rest," an opinion shared by R. E. Banta, who added that his importance as a poet was still to be evaluated.[3]

Thompson always regarded poetry as the highest type of literary art and his own poetry as his most significant work. He saw the poet as the highest type of man, one inspired to know and speak Truth and to deal, insofar as man can, with Beauty. He also saw the poet as a man marked by melancholy because he can never achieve all he aspires to.[4] All in all, it is a view that was old-fashioned even in Thompson's day, a view which owed a great deal to Shelley, Keats, and Poe.

His belief in the superiority of poetry over other forms of literature was doubtless the reason for his earliest work being in this form and for his regarding Howells' acceptance of a poem for the *Atlantic* in 1873 as the true beginning of his literary career, even though he had first published poems in *Scott's* in 1868 and had seen one poem published in the New York *Galaxy* eight months before the *Atlantic* poem. The *Atlantic* and Boston also represented for Thompson many qualities of the gentility to which he aspired, and this fact is another reason why he regarded publication in that journal as a landmark in his career. At any rate, when his poem "At the Window" attracted the attention and praise of both Howells and Longfellow, he began to feel more sure of a place in American poetry. He had sold two poems to *Lippincott's* and one to *Appleton's* during this year (1873), which also encouraged him. During the next few years he expanded his field to include *Harper's,* the *Independent, ·Scribner's,* and *Century.* By the early 1890's he was publishing in the *Critic, Cosmopolitan,* and *St. Nicholas* as well. After about 1883, the year in which Howells had written a very generous review of *Songs of Fair Weather* for the *Independent,* Thompson's poems tended more and more to concentrate in that magazine, and after he began his editorial association in 1889 the bulk of his work appeared there.

Thompson was not a prolific poet when compared to the other producers of verse in his period. Although he was a steady contributor, his name appeared far less frequently than those of Aldrich, Gilder, Stedman, Stoddard, Frank Dempster Sherman, Father Tabb, Louise Imogen Guiney, Mrs. Piatt, Ella Wheeler Wilcox, and Rose Terry Cooke. His three slender volumes, *Songs of Fair Weather* (1883), *Poems* (1892), of which the *Songs* constituted more than half, and *Lincoln's Grave* (1894), make a very slight showing against Gilder's sixteen volumes or Mrs. Wilcox's forty. Yet, though there may not be more gold in Thompson's work, by virtue of its spareness there is far less dross.

Thompson published just over 170 poems, most of these under one hundred lines in length. Nor is his range very wide: in his mature work he sang mainly of natural scenes, classical themes, domestic love, and patriotism. The poems of patriotism bulk large, although he had little of importance to say, and the forms are quite without distinction, except perhaps one poem on the theme of miscegenation. For the most part he eulogized Freedom, Union, and the Flag in stanzas such as the following:

America, new gospel bearer, hail!
  Thou second coming of the loving Lord!
Thy thousand years of glory cannot fail,
  Thou dewy, bloom-sweet resurrection of God's word![5]

In a series of poems called "Songs of the Mocking-Bird" he pursued the patriotic theme with an original but not very successful attempt at formal innovation. The poems purport to be the thoughts of the mockingbird—the democratic counterpart of the nightingale—and Thompson apparently sought to imitate in the metrical pattern the irregular phrasing of the mockingbird's song. The form has obvious kinships with the pseudo-Pindaric ode, but the result reads like a burlesque of that form. The extreme irregularity of the metrics is obtrusive in itself, and it is made even more obtrusive by the banality of what is being said. The first two stanzas of "In Captivity" will fairly represent these poems, being neither the worst nor the best:

    You ask me why
    I long to fly
Out from your palace to the dreamy woods
And the summer solitudes,
    Why I pine
    In this cage of mine,
    Why I fret,
    Why I set
All manner of querulous echoes fluttering forth
    From the cold North
And wandering Southward with beseeching pain
    In every strain.
    Ask me not
    Task me not
With such vain questions, but fling wide the door,
And hinder me no more;
Give back my wings to me,
And the wild currents of my liberty.[6]

The others celebrate, in much the same manner, the superiority of American over English and European institutions and the coming glory of American civilization, with a suggestion of the same anti-alien feeling that gave rise, at about this time, to Aldrich's "Unguarded Gates."

Both the Civil War and the Spanish-American War afforded themes and occasions for patriotic poetry, as did the pretentious Fourth of July celebrations (such as the one at Roseland Park), which were a standard feature of American culture during Thompson's life and after his death. When, in retrospect, he wrote of the Civil War it was usually to celebrate the new unity that the conflict brought to the country, at the same time not forgetting the "romantic" elements: the inspiring heroism of the soldiers and the pride and courage of their women-folk. In his long poem "Lincoln's Grave" he eulogized in the best patriotic mode of the time Lincoln's greatness as a man and as a leader, the glories of Freedom, the heroism of both the Blue and the Gray, and the glory of the new Union. The poem is a definitive expression of the middle-class American attitude of the 1890's toward the war. Occasionally he essayed a ballad, and with considerable success when he concentrated on the description of fast-moving action. "The Ballad of a Little Fun" is a good example.[7] Such a graphic touch as "a dying face / Scowled darkly at the sky," shows a talent for close observation and description. But on the whole the Civil War poems have little to distinguish them from reams of verse on the same subject by other versifiers of the period: they are simple statements of sentiment, sometimes embellished by pleasing or even striking images, expressed in simple traditional forms—four and five stress couplets and quatrains in varying combinations and minor variations.

The Fourth of July poems are even less distinguished but at the same time were eminently well gauged to the audience for which they were intended. Although there is no way of knowing what Thompson's attitude toward them was, it is likely that he regarded them not so much as poetry but as verses produced on a commission for an occasion: the fact that one of them is in dialect ("The Bloom o' the World") supports this thesis, since he did not regard dialect verse as a form of poetry. Lacking distinction, these poems are not without interest, however, because they show Thompson leaning toward that curious combination of frightened insularity and aggressive nationalism which characterized American imperialism toward the end of the century. If foreign "anarchists" do not like our institutions, he said, they should go back where they came

from. And when he came to cry America's virtues he was apt to give
an important place to military strength. In a poem for *America,*
1891, after eulogizing a certain abstract Freedom and Liberty, he
said:

> Let dull aristocrats reprove
> And at our fervor sneer;
> They never saw our armies move,
> Or heard our soldiers cheer.[8]

His poems on the Spanish-American War and the problems leading up to it show him fulfilling this early tendency and vociferously
embracing the imperialist position. As early as 1895 he called for
the liberation of Cuba:

> Poor, drowning Cuba grips our skirt,—
> Shall Freedom shake her off?
>
> O no! fling out the fleet and flag,
> To shield her from the storm,
> And let that splendid island feel
> The clasp of Freedom's arm.[9]

And once the war was fought he was for the permanent annexation
of Cuba and the maximum extension of American colonial power,
not on a merely practical basis, but as the verdict of Destiny. In
our blood, he said, runs "the true imperial strain" inherited from
mother England.[10] Our great battleships are "making good the
imperial right/ Of our race to the mastery and the lead."[11] And,
finally, it was his fervent conviction that God urges us on:

> Follow the pillared cloud of war, flame-shot against the blue,
> With Glory's banner overhung, God has his eye on you;
> God who did lead His host of old through battle-din and death,
> Who smote His foes with carnage-blows and burnt them in His
> breath,
> Is calling you to meet the storm, He hails you in His might,
> And over all the earth shall lie the harvest of the fight;
> Hail! Hail! O masters of the glaive, O spearmen brave and true;
> Hail! reapers of the reeking swath, God has His eye on you.[12]

Thompson's Civil War experiences might be pointed out as the
source of this defense of violence. If the "Ballad of a Little Fun"

is any indication, he certainly knew and took pleasure in reliving the exhilaration of close combat, the emotional abandon that is possible in pursuit of an immediate life-or-death object. But he could not have been a soldier without also knowing the physical and mental miseries that go along with and make up a far greater part of the soldier's life than do the heroic moments. That he chose to forget the miseries (so far as I can find, he never once mentions them in either poetry or prose) and to emphasize the glories admits of several explanations. The social sanctions attaching to violence, particularly the military variety, in the South of Thompson's boyhood probably had something to do with it. His military service at a highly impressionable age when a little excitement makes up for a great deal of discomfort probably served to reinforce this early training. Even his early religious training may be obscurely involved: the Primitive Baptist ideas of divine election and of a just but sometimes violent God certainly would not be in conflict with the imperialist attitude. In his poetry, he out-Beveridged Senator Beveridge in his vociferous demands for expansion, demands based on a belief in America's messianic role, with war as an implement if necessary.[13]

His ideas about America's destiny have a strong taint of racism, so it is not surprising to find the same taint when he writes of domestic issues—the Negro problem in particular. It is widely acknowledged that one of the most important factors in the North-South reconciliation after the Civil War was the partial acceptance of the southern attitude toward the Negro by the North and West. After the humanitarian flurry of the Abolition movement had died down, the Anglo-Saxon cultists and certain economic groups with whom the Negro could compete found it convenient to keep him in an inferior status. This was done in part by asserting that the Negro was an inferior race and that miscegenation, the inevitable outgrowth of social equality, represented a real danger to the future of the country. In this cry Thompson was one of the loudest—so loud, in fact, that he shocked Richard Watson Gilder with his poem "A Voodoo Prophecy," in which he foresaw a vengeful dominance by the black race sometime in the future.

> I am the prophet of the dusky race,
>   The poet of wild Africa. Behold,

The midnight vision brooding in my face!
    Come near me,
    And hear me,
  While from my lips the words of Fate are told.

The song I sing is rank as jungle-weeds
  And noxious as the deadly viper's breath;
Its wafts are clouded with the winged seeds
    And anther dust
    And poison-must
  Blown from the odorous garden-lands of Death.

A black and terrible memory masters me,
  The shadow and the substance of deep wrong;
You know the past, hear now what is to be;
    From the midnight land,
    Over sea and sand
  From the green jungle hear my Voodoo-song:

A tropic heat is in my bubbling veins,
  Quintessence of all savagery is mine,
The lust of ages ripens in my reins,
    And burns
    And yearns,
  Like venom-sap within a noxious vine.

Was I a heathen? Ay, I was—am still
  A fetich [sic] worshipper; but I was free
To loiter or to wander at my will,
    To leap and dance,
    To hurl my lance,
  And breathe the air of savage liberty.

Sweet was the thoughtless current of my life,
  And dear my hut beside the silent stream;
I loved my children and my comely wife,
    In savage fashion,
    With fervent passion;
  But now it all is distant as a dream.

You drew me to a higher life, you say;
  Ah, drove me with the lash of slavery!

Am I unmindful? Every cursed day
   Of pain
   And chain
Roars like a torrent in my memory.

You make my manhood whole with 'equal rights'!
   Poor empty words! Dream you I honor them?—
I who have stood on Freedom's wildest hights? [*sic*]
   My Africa,
   I see the day
When none dare touch thy garment's lowest hem.

You gave me manhood? Was it yours to give?
   Where are my forest and my cool, deep stream?—
And where the hut in which my wife did live?
   My children wild—
   Show me one child
Of all the dear ones crowding in my dreams.

You cannot make me love you with your whine
   Of fine repentance. Veil your pallid face
In presence of the shame that mantles mine;
   Stand
   At command
Of the black prophet of the Negro race!

My brain is heavy with dark memories
   Of hopeless days and nights surcharged with wrong,
When in your vessel, sailing over seas,
   I tried my chain
   With furious strain,
And raved because my life would last so long.

You boast that your pure touch has aided me,
   Has brought me to a clearer, sweeter air;
Go tell that to the dumb fish of the sea,
   That writhe and die
   When drawn on high
And cast upon the shore-land green and fair!

Your schools, your books, can they wash off the stain
   Set by long centuries of servitude?

What should I be, even if you made me white?
   A faded slave
   A bleachèd knave,
Whose face would tell his origin low and lewd.

Preach not to me, I know you to the core;
   Was it not you who lashed my bleeding back?
Is it not you who tramp from shore to shore
     Of a free land
     With gun and brand
Leaving the stench of slaughter in your track?

I hate you, and I live to nurse my hate,
   Remembering when you plied the slaver's trade
In my dear land. . . . How patiently I wait
     The day
     Not far away,
When all your pride shall shrivel up and fade.

Yea, all your whiteness darken under me!
   Darken and be jaundiced, and your blood
Take in dread humors from my savagery,
     Until
     Your will
Lapse into mine and seal my masterhood.

You, race of God, made out of fairer clay,
   Whose nostrils caught the breath of high emprise
Hear me, while I your future doom foresay—
     Hear me
     And fear me,
For dreams of torture hover in mine eyes.

You, seed of Abel, proud of your descent,
   And arrogant, because your cheeks are fair,
Within my loins an inky curse is pent
     To flood
     Your blood
And stain your skin and crisp your golden hair.

You whitened sepulcher, can you deny
   That you filled me with nameless dreams of lust?

Can I forget them—will they ever die?
  Their fire
  Burns higher, higher,
  While lash and manacle are rusting into dust.

I have your precepts graven in my heart,
  Sweet science of all evil steeped in pride,
Lewdness and lechery gilded with fine art,
    And the bloom
    And perfume
  Of sin in shame held close and glorified.

As you have done by me, so will I do
  By all the generations of your race;
Your snowy limbs, your blood's patrician blue
    Shall be
    Tainted by me,
  And I will set my seal upon your face!

Yea, I will dash my blackness down your veins,
  And through your nerves my sensuousness I'll fling;
Your lips, your eyes, shall bear the musty stains
    Of Congo kisses
    While shrieks and hisses
  Shall blend into the savage songs I sing!

Your temples will I break, your fountains fill,
  Your cities raze, your fields to deserts turn;
My heathen fires shall shine on every hill,
    And wild beasts roam,
    Where stands your home;—
  Even the wind your hated dust shall spurn.

I will absorb your very life in me,
  And mold you to the shape of my desire;
Back through the cycles of all cruelty
    I will swing you,
    And wring you,
  And roast you in my passions' hottest fire.

You, North and South, you, East and West,
  Shall drink the cup your fathers gave to me;

My back still burns, I bare my bleeding breast,
> I set my face,
> My limbs I brace,
To make the long, strong fight for mastery.

My serpent fetich [*sic*] lolls its withered lip
> And bares its shining fangs at thought of this;
I scarce can hold the monster in my grip,
> So strong is he,
> So eagerly
He leaps to meet my precious prophecies.

Hark for the coming of my countless host,
> Watch for my banner over land and sea.
The ancient power of vengeance is not lost!
> Lo! on the sky
> The fire-clouds fly,
And strangely moans the windy, weltering sea.

It is not long to wait; the tide is swift
> Adown the channel leading to my goal;
To that dread focus all the currents drift!
> Back once more
> To Afric's shore
The waves of human destiny darkly roll.

Roll, billows! bear me swiftlier on and on—
> Oh, fiends in white, teach me a little more,
The while my limbs wax to resistless brawn,
> And in my heart
> The avenger's art
Is mastered and remastered o'er and o'er.

Even now a waft comes in from censers swung
> By grimy hands in twilight gathering fast;
Hark what wild notes from savage throats are rung!
> Out be the light!
> Hail to the night!
Thou, Prince of Darkness, rule the world at last!

Thompson had sent the poem to Gilder in August of 1889 with the hope of getting it in the *Century*. Gilder promptly returned it, objecting that it blurted itself forth in statements of disagreeable truth, that the form as well as the content was too rough, and that, if for no other reason, he could not publish it because of possible political repercussions.[14] Thompson defended both the sentiments and the strength of the poem, adding that he was haunted by the need to get his message before the public to the extent that he would publish the poem privately if he could find no other outlet. However, he finally published it in the *Independent* early in 1892.[15]

Thompson's insistence on the strength of this poem, although he regretted its roughness when compared to the "chaste and spiritual" lyrics of Gilder, may have been the result merely of his intense concern with the material of it. Still he would have been right in claiming for it an unusual achievement in form if that were the grounds of his admiration. The poem is weakened by an obtrusive and patched-out rhyme scheme, and its meter is rough and irregular if measured by the standards which Gilder and Thompson probably applied to it; but in this roughness Thompson built better than he knew. Here are foreshadowings of the syncopated rhythms which Vachel Lindsay was to use two decades later in dealing with the Afro-American in "The Congo." The adumbrations are faint, and it is doubtful that Thompson consciously attempted an African rhythm, because of the frequent triumph of the iambic; but such lines as "I am the prophet of the dusky race" and "Yea, I will dash my blackness down your veins," and "The midnight vision brooding in my face" and "You, seed of Abel, proud of your descent" suggest a rhythm peculiarly appropriate to the matter and the narrator.

There is, moreover, a marked ambivalence of tone that gives a depth and power unusual for Thompson's work. There is sympathy for the Negro as victim of the personal degradation that goes with slavery; there is scorn for those white men who degraded and debauched the Negro and for the system which allowed these evils; and there is a revulsion from, an abhorrence of, the Negro and the culture he supposedly will bring with him. This revulsion is expressed mainly in sexual terms either directly stated (lust . . . in my reins; Congo kisses; within my loins an inky curse. . . .) or disguised as serpent imagery (song - viper's breath; the lust is "like venom-sap within a noxious vine"; "My serpent fetich [*sic*] lolls its withered lip . . . I scarce can hold the monster in my grip"). This triple attitude is thus far wonderfully expressive of the approved sentiments of no small segment of "enlightened" and humanitarian Victorians. Thompson was willing to admit that the Negro had suffered a grievous wrong at the hands of the white race, but the thought of allowing the half-savage Negro, as an atonement, to "pollute" the blood of the white race was to him both unreasonable and intolerable.[16]

The vehemence of the indictment against the white Christian and the pervasiveness of serpent imagery carrying a tone of horrible fascination suggest an emotional involvement on Thompson's part which a psychologist might profitably pursue. Likewise, his stubborn defense of the poem against Gilder's strictures and his determination to get it published regardless of cost suggest that for him it had an importance beyond its statement about the Negro problem. But for whatever reasons, the poem represents for Thompson an unusual accomplishment in its rhythms, diction, and complexity.

In contrast to the poems of patriotism, the poems on classical themes seem to be almost wholly lifeless, formal exercises. They are facile, smooth, simple, and apparently quite disconnected from the life of the times. In one poem Thompson complained that Aoede, an obscure lyric muse, kept eluding him and longed to see him die. He wrote a series of sonnets descriptive of Eros, Aphrodite, Psyche, and Persephone; he described Diana in a series of couplets ranging from the competent to the ridiculous.[17] In one poem to Ceres he created a highly effective contrast between the classical dream and the midwestern actuality by means of breaking off his reverie thus:

> A clash and clang. "Go 'long, Red-buck!"
> Late from their work my boys had come,
> And drowned the goddess' song the while
> They hauled a broken harrow home.[18]

But when he included it in his collected poems he cut off this life-giving stanza. His most ambitious classical exercise was a translation in blank verse of the Seventh Idyl of Theocritus. The blank verse is competent, though frequent inversions and patching out of lines are noticeable. Thompson offered it to Gilder for the *Century* saying that he intended to dedicate it to Stedman,[19] but he was evidently rebuffed by both because he finally published it in the *Independent* and dedicated it to Professor Charles Forster Smith of Vanderbilt University.[20]

His only other major effort at translation was another of the mockingbird songs, "To Sappho," in which he attempted to weave translations of the Sapphic fragments through the bird's running commentary on Life and Liberty and Love.

It is hard to escape the impression in reading these classical poems that the writing of them was more an escape from life than an interpretation of it. Although Thompson's familiarity with the Greek pastoral tradition may have had some effect on his own nature poetry, his concern in later life with classical themes and translations seems more a badge of conspicuous leisure, in the Veblenian sense. These poems represent an occupation not concerned with pecuniary reward and stand as a symbol of the genteel life to which Thompson always aspired. A knowledge of Greek literature was one of the signs of the *ancien régime,* which to his mind was the guardian of the cultural tradition which was in danger of being lost. The study of Greek and the writing of poems on classical themes then became an act of allegiance to the old values. The ceremonial and emotional character of the interest is further indicated in that it did not include the dramatists and philosophers, the writers who grapple with the really important problems of human existence. It may also have been pure and simple escape into a realm that offered no problems, in which values were certain and life was simple. He said almost as much in his little piece "Written on a Fly-Leaf of Theocritus";

> One could be sure of something then
> Severely simple, simply grand,
> Or keenly, subtly sweet, as when
> Venus and Love went hand in hand.[21]

The lyrics of domestic love reflect a life eminently respectable and tranquil. They are of such an even and bloodless tenor, so marked by sentiment rather than passion, that one suspects them of being mere conventional expressions—not in the sense of being insincere but in the sense of being limited by convention to the expression of sentiment rather than passion. For even passion between man and wife was by common consent of the genteel poets a secret thing, not the material for poetry. Thompson stayed well within the permissible limits and also well within traditional forms. His poems are simple statements in verse of genuine affection for his wife and children, a strong domesticity. Like most of his patriotic poems, these are not distinguishable from the myriad competently turned magazine poems of the period on the same themes. A stanza from one of his favorites will amply illustrate:

> Sweet little Jessie, two years old,
>   Dear little Mamma, twenty-four,
> Together in the garden walk
>   While evening sun-streams round them pour.
> List! Mamma murmurs baby-talk!
>   Hush! Jessie's talk to laughter glows!
> They both look heavenly sweet to me,
>   Between the poppy and the rose.[22]

The nature poems are the one vein in which he might be said to be consistently more than commonplace, even distinguished. This distinction lies partly in the freshness of subject, vocabulary, and metaphor—his range was the flora and fauna of the southern United States, hitherto unexploited in a realistic manner; it lies partly in his talent for compact, graphic descriptions, particularly of action; and it lies partly in the emotional intensity he sometimes achieved. He never succeeded in intellectualizing the natural scene, in using natural figures and images to carry a philosophical burden, as Emerson did[23] —never tried to, in fact. But within their narrow limits the poems are effective.

Since well over half of Thompson's poetry would fall in this category, it is not easy to do it justice in a short selection. But perhaps four items will give a sufficient idea of the characteristics of this vein.[24]

"The Fawn" describes a hunting incident in semi-lyrical fashion:

> I lay close down beside the river,
> My bow well strung, well-filled my quiver.
>
> The god that dwells among the reeds
> Sang sweetly from their tangled bredes;
>
> The soft-tongued water murmured low,
> Swinging the flag-leaves to and fro.
>
> Beyond the river, fold on fold,
> The hills gleamed through a film of gold;

The feathery osiers waved and shone
Like silver threads in tangles blown.

A bird, fire-winged, with ruby throat,
Down the slow, drowsy wind did float,

And drift and flit and stay along,
A very focal flame of song.

A white sand-isle amid the stream
Lay sleeping by its shoals of bream;

In lilied pools, alert and calm,
Great bass through lucent circles swam;

And farther, by a rushy brink,
A shadowy fawn stole down to drink,

Where tall, thin birds unbalanced stood
In sandy shallows of the flood.

And what did I beside the river,
With bow well-strung and well-filled quiver?

I lay quite still with half-closed eyes,
Lapped in a dream of Paradise,

Until I heard a bow-cord ring,
And from the reeds an arrow sing.

I knew not of my brother's luck,
If well or ill his shaft had struck;

But something in his merry shout
Put my sweet summer dream to rout,

And up I sprang, with bow half-drawn,
And keen desire to slay the fawn.

But where was it? Gone like my dream.
I only heard the fish-hawk scream,

And the strong striped bass leap up
Beside the lily's floating cup;

I only felt the cool wind go
Across my face with steady flow;

I only saw those thin birds stand
Unbalanced on the river sand,

Low peering at some dappled thing
In the green rushes quivering.

The natural scene is fairly well realized in terms of "feathery
osiers," "shoals of bream," and "tall, thin birds." There is a certain
dramatic effect in the contrast between the dream mood of the
first part and the tense, active mood of the second. But the
originality and effectiveness of the poem lie mainly in its quasi-
savage overtones—"a keen desire to slay the fawn." In the final
couplet describing the dying animal he has committed a kind of
fascinating mayhem on the traditional sentimentality toward fawns
and has pointed up the very graphic image with a striking rhyme.

"A Prelude" reflects an interesting attempt to utilize metaphor
organically rather than decoratively.

Spirit that moves the sap in spring,
When lusty male birds fight and sing,
Inform my words, and make my lines
As sweet as flowers, as strong as vines.

Let mine be the freshening power
Of rains on grass, of dew on flower;
The fertilizing song be mine,
Nut-flavored, racy, keen as wine.

Let some procreant truth exhale
From me before my forces fail;
Or ere the ecstatic impulse go,
Let all my buds to blossoms blow.

If quick, sound seed be wanting where
The virgin soil feels sun and air,
And longs to fill a higher state,
There let my meanings germinate.

Let not my strength be spilled for naught,
But, in some fresher vessel caught,
Be blended into sweeter forms,
And fraught with purer aims and charms.

Let bloom-dust of my life be blown
To quicken hearts that flower alone;
Around my knees let scions rise
With heavenward-pointed destinies.

And when I fall, like some old tree,
And subtile change makes mould of me,
There let earth show a fertile line
Whence perfect wild-flowers leap and shine.

To say that he wanted to be a fertilizing, seminal influence,
Thompson chose a series of figures: he is rain, dew, seed, a growing
tree, pollen, and finally a fallen tree making a fertile line in the
earth as it decays. Although these figures separately seem appro-
priately related to the theme, the unified progression is broken by
the fifth stanza and the poem falls short of organic wholeness.

In "Spring's Torch-Bearer," Thompson attempts the elaboration
of a single metaphor, building the poem around the figure of the
oriole as a torch.

Oriole—athlete of the air—
    Of fire and song a glowing core,
From tropic wildernesses fair,
    Spring's favorite lampadephore.

A hot flambeau on either wing
    Rimples as you pass me by;
'Tis seeing flame to hear you sing,
    'Tis hearing song to see you fly.

Below the leaves in fragrant gloom,
    Cool currents lead you to your goal,
Where bursting jugs of rich perfume
    Down honeyed slopes of verdure roll.

In eddies, round some hummock cold,
    Where violets weave their azure bredes,
You flash a torch o'er rimy mould
    And rouse the dormant balsam seeds.

Upon the sassafras a flare,
    And through the elm a wavering sheen,
A flicker in the orchard fair,
    A flame across the hedgerow green.

Your voice and light are in my dream
    Of vanished youth, they warm my heart;
With every chirrup, every gleam,
    Sweet currents from old fountains start.

I take me wings and fly with you,
    Once more the boy of long ago.
Oh, days of bloom! Oh, honey-dew!
    Hark! how the flutes of fairy blow!

You whisk wild splendors through the trees,
    And send keen fervors down the wind,
You singe the jackets of the bees,
    And trail an opal mist behind.

When flowery hints foresay the berry,
    On spray of haw and tuft of brier,
Then, wandering incendiary,
    You set the maple swamps afire!

As in "A Prelude" the orderly progress of the poem is broken, in this case by two stanzas that ignore the torch figure and focus attention on the poet's recollections of his youth. But in spite of the intrusion of stanzas six and seven, the poem is rather striking for its elaboration of the bird-torch metaphor in images such as "opal mist" and flaming maple swamp and in rhymes such as "glowing core . . . lampadephore" and "foresay the berry . . . incendiary."

Perhaps Thompson's most effective poem is "The Assault," subtitled *"Amazilia Cerviniventris"* (Buff-bellied Hummingbird).

A winged rocket, curving through
    An amethyst trajectory,
Blew up the magazines of dew
    Within the fortress of the bee.

Some say the tulip mortar sent
    The missile forth; I do not know;
I scarcely saw the way it went,
    Its whisk of flame surprised me so.

I heard the sudden hum and boom,
    And saw the arc of purple light

> Across the garden's rosy gloom;
>   Then something glorious blurred my sight!
>
> The bees forgot to sound alarm,
>   And did not pause their gates to lock;
> A topaz terror took by storm
>   The tower of the hollyhock.
>
> Above the rose a halo hung,
>   As if a bomb had been a gem,
> And round the dahlia's head was swung
>   A blade that looked a diadem.
>
> What more befell I cannot say;
>   By ruby glint and emerald gleam
> My sense was dazed; the garden lay
>   Around me like an opal dream!

Although a variety of images appear—the bird is variously a projectile, an assaulting force, and a sword—they are all presented under the central metaphor of the garden-fortress under attack. The fresh, vivid imagery, the tone of unsophisticated delight in nature, and the subject matter are suggestive of Emily Dickinson's "A Route of Evanescence."[25]

Such a summary as this, while describing the more important categories of Thompson's work, is in danger of slighting the less important, such as religious poems and children's poems. But these do not alter the notable fact about Thompson's poetry as a whole, namely, that spiritual uncertainty, the search for new values in a changing world—that pervasive theme of the great Victorian poets— never appeared. If he realized the ambiguities of life that appeared to certain of his contemporaries or if he seriously explored the spiritual implications of nineteenth-century science or the cultural implications of the post-Civil War economic development, his poetry does not indicate it. Such narrowness does not necessarily deny greatness to the artist, though breadth of vision is always a point in his favor. But whether or not this lack of breadth explains his limitations as a poet, the reasons for it and for certain other qualities of his poetry are essentially the same ones that influenced his criticism: rigid moral and religious views, the sin-sex identification, and the aspiration toward genteel status. Thus it was natural that he found his models for the most part in the tradition of Longfellow, Lowell, Whittier, and the Ideal poets of his own generation.

Not to be ignored as a shaping force was the poetic market. If one wanted to sell poetry to *Atlantic* and *Century* one had to meet the taste of the editors. One way was to imitate what had already met it. Undoubtedly this was done by a great many versifiers, probably more piously than cynically. In addition, Thompson was loud in his belief that an author ought to be a business man who tailored his product to the market.[26] The general effect of such a situation was obviously conservative; it tended to keep the aspiring but impecunious poet in the Longfellow-Whittier tradition.

All these limiting and stultifying factors were part of the civilized life which Thompson revered. At the same time he savored life in wild nature because it offered him a refuge from the frustrations of civilization. In this paradox probably lies the explanation for the relative superiority of his nature poetry. In this area freshness and originality were possible, if realized with only moderate success.

As would be expected, the contemporary reception of Thompson's poetry was somewhat more favorable, despite certain negative opinions, than a twentieth-century estimate can be. When his first volume appeared, the critical attitudes were mixed, varying from genuine enthusiasm to clear distaste, from *Harper's* verdict that here was a new Theocritus to the Chicago *Dial's* feeling that here was "poverty of poetry."[27] Most of the reviewers took a middle ground, agreeing that the nature poems were fresh, graphic, vigorous, delightful but that as a poet Thompson lacked depth, emotional intensity, technical ease. The obtrusiveness of his rhyme and the occasional purposeless forcing of a rhyme were commented upon. Thompson must have taken some comfort from the fact that the magazines that really mattered for him, the *Atlantic,* the *Century,* and the *Independent,* were all favorable.[28] In fact, Howells' glowing review in the *Independent* was probably the strongest praise Thompson ever received: "Delicately graceful, full of a fresh new speech for Nature. . . . Nothing more Western than this sensitively refined and lovely verse has yet come from the West. . . . Here there is something as fine as it is free, as gentle as it is native, as elect as it is wild in flavor, as lawful as it is sylvan in spirit. . . . Here, in a word, are conscious and instinctive art allied to a love of nature, the most simple and joyous and unaffected that has for many a year found voice in rhyme." How much the rather warm personal friendship between the two men at this time had to do with Howells' estimate of the poetry there is no way of knowing, but quite apart from the friendship, this was the type of poetry that Howells appreciated; it was much like his own.

When *Poems* appeared nineteen years later, the extremes of both praise and censure were missing, and the general tenor of the comments is remarkably close to the median opinion of *Songs of Fair Weather*—probably because most of the critics agreed that the best poems of the volume were those which had made up the body of its predecessor.[29] Perhaps because *Poems* represented no essentially new achievement, perhaps because Howells had been alienated by Thompson's public abuse, the older man gave the book no public welcome.

Thompson's last volume, *Lincoln's Grave,* received very little notice. The *Independent*'s was the only review that could be called flattering. The reviewer found in each line "severe completeness, . . . each word fitted to its place and carrying its load of color or of form" and believed that there was "nothing to compare with it in our poetry" since Whitman's "O Captain! My Captain!" The Indianapolis *News* called it a "poem of permanent value," and the *Critic,* without specifying, said it had "at least one passage of power and beauty." William Morton Payne, in the *Dial,* bestowed a backhanded compliment when he admitted that it was "dignified, worthy of the subject and occasion, and soars to a higher flight than any of which we had thought the writer capable."[30]

Another index to the extent and quality of Thompson's popularity is the degree to which his poems were anthologized. Beginning with Longfellow's inclusion of "The Wabash" in *Poems of Places* (1879), Thompson found a place from time to time in various genteel anthologies as late as 1923. The most notable of these were *The Cambridge Book of Poetry and Song,* edited by Charlotte F. Bates (1882), *American Sonnets,* edited by T. W. Higginson and E. H. Bigelow (1900), and Stedman's *American Anthology* (1900). In these anthologies the nature poems were steadily popular, and after the inflammatory nationalism of the 1890's the patriotic poems began to attract notice.

In perspective, then, Thompson appears as a poet with severe limitations in several senses. His intellectual vision was circumscribed by a narrow and defensive religious commitment as well as by his geographical, social, and economic situation. His emotional nature was oppressed by moral taboos. His life was so rigidly set in an authoritarian framework that he could never let spiritual conflicts into the conscious realm, could never cultivate those arguments with himself which are one source of great poetry. His technical abilities were also largely limited by his reverence for tradition and authority. Although his critical dicta were not always reverent, his acts of poetic expression were. Even his apparent innovations in the "Songs of 'the Mocking-Bird" were essentially superficial: he merely modified the pseudo-Pindaric form to make it somewhat more irregular than earlier writers had made it. It was only from his contact with nature—the area of experience in which he achieved a certain emotional expression and release from the limiting aspects of his existence—that he was able to make poetry of a fresher-than-average sort.

CHAPTER V

THE FICTION WRITER

THOMPSON'S REGULAR PRODUCTION of nature essays, poetry, and criticism, combined with his law practice up to 1884 and his heavy editorial duties after 1889, might seem to have left little time for anything else; nevertheless, he produced a fairly steady stream of fiction. It may well be that he had good grounds for writing to Richard Watson Gilder, "You have no idea how prolific I am; . . . I believe I can do more work than any man I ever saw. . . ."[1] Beginning in the late 1860's with contributions to *Scott's* and continuing in the 1870's with the Hoosier stories that make up *Hoosier Mosaics* (1875), he published seven novels (two in serial form) during the 1880's, three novels during the 1890's, and two other novels immediately prior to his death. In addition, during the twenty years preceding his death he published a number of local-color stories, six of which were collected in 1898 as *Stories of the Cherokee Hills,* and more than a dozen stories in a sometimes-sensational vein of historical romance. Again, it is a small showing in comparison with the output of a really prolific writer like Howells, but considering the press of Thompson's other duties, it is quite a respectable one—in bulk, at least.

It is convenient, for the purpose of surveying Thompson's fiction, to divide it into five general types, although it should be understood that these do not always appear in isolation. Perhaps it would be more accurate to say, if we mark off a small amount of fiction for juveniles as a type that has little relevance to his serious work, that there are four important strains which run through his fic-

116

tion: quasi-Gothic romance; southern and Hoosier local color; genteel romance of contemporary life, with hints of Howellsian realism; and swashbuckling historical romance.

The juvenile fiction, though it attests to his continuous interest in young people, was clearly written to order and didactic in purpose. Only two items are of any length—both short novels. "Marvin and His Boy Hunters" contains, in addition to the adventure yarn, a rather full course of instruction on the care and use of firearms in hunting.[2] *The Ocala Boy* is the story of the reception of two northern lads in a Florida town, and it owes its existence in book form to the fact that the Lothrop Publishing Company of Boston found itself with the manuscript on its hands after selling its *Wide-Awake* magazine to *St. Nicholas*, having contracted for the story with the intention of publishing it serially in *Wide-Awake*.[3] A shorter piece is a simplified version of some of the Robin Hood stories, an outgrowth of his interest in archery.[4]

In Thompson's serious fiction the Gothic strain dominates his earliest novel, "The Mill of God," although by locating the action on the St. John's River, with part of it taking place on the Jacksonville waterfront, he also made use of southern local color. However, the action revolves around a dark and mysterious man, an English nobleman in voluntary exile, with an equally mysterious entourage, living amid oriental opulence in a forest-embowered retreat called Castle Splendor. He is a student of the occult arts of the mysterious East and is loved by a Semitic princess, a woman of supernatural powers who is able to foretell and arrange the future. Under her guidance, and with the help of an Arab named Donald, the nobleman is reconciled with his long-lost sons, the mistake that caused the estrangement is cleared up, and the whole party is saved from the vengeance of a horrid dwarf named Monster, whose pedigree is unique: "His father was a mulatto and his mother the daughter of two intellectual, physical and moral deformities, her father being a dwarf-giant of monstrous passions and utterly depraved soul, and her mother being a hideous, toothless, sightless thing of a nature too dark, and of parentage too horrible to be here mentioned. It is sufficient to say that if the story is true, the dwarf Monster had in his veins the blood of the most depraved humanity mingling with that of the ourangoutang [sic] and a certain serpent whose existence is yet doubted by naturalists."[5]

Behind this flamboyance of plot and character there is a

crude and imitative attempt at symbolism in the mode of Hawthorne, an attempt which reflects, however, only the most superficial understanding of Hawthorne's technique: Thompson made
Monster the embodiment of evil and Donald, in flagrant imitation
of Donatello, the embodiment of moral innocence, or moral ignorance.[6] But these qualities are not related in any functional
way to the other characters or to the action. In short, the moral
symbolism, if we may call it that, is developed purely as an
exhibition of virtuosity.

In later years Thompson was not eager to acknowledge his auth-
orship of "The Mill of God." He never mentioned it, but he did
mention another of his early novels—he was forced to—in mock
horror. "The League of the Guadalupe" was written about the
same time as "The Mill of God" and in the same vein; he sold
it to Street and Smith's New York *Weekly* for $100 in 1870 and
forgot about it. But in 1889 he discovered it "all dripping with
gore," being serialized in the *Weekly*.[7]

In his later fiction, although the Gothic strain is never dominant, it is frequently present. In both of his long historical romances he used a dwarf for a minor character, but neither is so
sinister as Monster; and in each of these stories there is as well
a major character that might be described as Gothic. Max Burns,
in *The King of Honey Island*, becomes almost a zombie through his
monomaniac desire to kill Pierre Rameau. Several times he is
left for dead, but his monomania carries him on, apparently without
food or shelter, until the moment when he and his victim die
together. In the character of the Indian, Long-Hair, in *Alice of
Old Vincennes*, the supernatural overtones are lacking, i.e., he is
not sustained or motivated by an occult force, but his savagery,
his cruelty, his physical endurance are superhuman. An example
of the Gothic strain among the shorter pieces is "Banzou Jean."
Here the narrator finds himself deep in the Louisiana swamps with
reason to believe that the original proprietor of the cabin he is
occupying—an escaped slave who was a voodoo priest—is exerting
some occult influence over him.[8]

Next to appear was the local-color strain, in *Hoosier Mosaics*.[9]
These stories exhibit close attention to the realization of the
particular locale in terms of natural scenery, a generally sentimental
concept of human nature (still allowing for some very rough ex-
teriors), and a generally realistic record of manners, dress, and

speech—all of which are characteristic of the local-color technique as it was then being practiced by Harte, Cable, Eggleston, Johnston, and others.[10] In fact, in describing the natural scene it would appear that Thompson sometimes forgot that he was not writing a nature essay, to the detriment of the action. As to human nature, there are characters in three different stories pining away from disappointment in love, while another nobly joins the girl he loves to her city lover but makes a periodical pilgrimage, for the sake of his old love, to the place "whar I fust seed the gal."[11] In another instance, Miss Susie Adair, the Venus of Balhinch, unable to return the affections of a young Ichabod who has called on her, suppresses her desire to laugh at him, which would be too cruel, but then pours a churn of buttermilk over his head and thinks it the best joke in the world. This strange combination of sentimentality and practical jokery would suggest that Thompson was not blind to a certain earthy strain in Hoosier manners. Such an assumption is borne out by other very realistic and un-genteel descriptions: for instance, at an inn the landlord's "little sharp-nosed, weasel-eyed boy" spoke for the gizzard of the chicken that was being served, and when he got it "he turned his head on one side and ate like a cat."[12] But when comedy is not the primary object, characterization is according to the canons of the sentimental tradition.

Dialect, of course, is one of the most important features of this strain. It is pervasive in *Hoosier Mosaics,* and convincingly handled, as it is in the rather infrequent Hoosier stories that appeared later; but it is Thompson's stories of the southern mountains that mark him as a true artist in dialect, as well as a loving historian of a vanishing culture. The locale is the Cherokee hill country of his boyhood. According to his introduction to *Stories of the Cherokee Hills,* he began consciously to study its literary possibilities when he returned home after the Civil War; he began to write the stories about the same time but found that editors in the early 1870's were hostile to them in the belief that " 'fiction in any way connected with the recent war in the South and its results' could not fail to 'engender ill feeling and do injury to both writer and publisher.' "[13] If the editors also added that Thompson's unblushing advocacy of white supremacy in the stories would not have been well-received by the North at that time, he did not mention it in his account of the circumstances surrounding their publication.

But the fact remains that most of the stories did not get into print until the 1890's, by which time the North had become reconciled to the southern point of view.

Except for two stories, "A Dusky Genius" and "A Race Romance," in which Thompson pursued his crochet about the eventual domination of the white by the black race, he eschewed the role of propagandist for that of historian of the southern mountain culture. There are close descriptions of the geography and architecture as well as studies of speech and social forms and folk songs. Of course he tended to emphasize the unusual, the picturesque aspects, such as the almost brotherly relationship between Ben and Judas, master and slave suckled at the same breast and constant companions from infancy to dotage; or the highly competitive and enjoyable thieving that went on between two cracker families living on opposite sides of a mountain; or the unregenerate and original attitude of a certain Bud Peavey, who had been such a consistent and enthusiastic sinner all his life that he was genuinely affronted when it appeared to him that the devil had gone back on their long friendship. But in the process of recounting these unusual stories Thompson succeeded remarkably well in giving life to a large cast of characters, in portraying their manners, their speech, their persons. Certain of them, like Bud Peavey and Daddy Kirkendall, the "hirsute, corrugated," mountain preacher, appeared in several of the stories, but it is in "A Friend to the Devil" that Bud Peavey appears at his best—earthy, domineering, shrewd: " 'I air boss of these yer diggin's an' they air goin' ter take th'r med'cine w'enever I say fer 'em to. Ef any feller don't jes' like my way o' doin', w'y jes' let 'im mention it, an' I'll climb his frame an' mek er gin'ral ramshak of 'im afore he kin grunt. That's w'at I'll do; an' I'll do it s'prisin' quick, too.' "[14] Here, too, appeared the best of the numerous folk songs that Thompson recorded, this breakdown verse, for instance:

> How d'ye do, ole Uncle Nick?
> Gi' me a swaller o' hot lead, quick!
> Soak me good in b'ilin' ile,
> An' smooth me off wi' er red-hot file![15]

During the 1890's, he returned to the Hoosier milieu only twice, but it was vastly different from the rather primitive and backwoodsy society that he had dealt with twenty years earlier. The more interesting of these stories, entitled "Smithers," is set against the backdrop of prosperous Indiana farm life.[16] It has the dialect and the usual descriptions that one expects of the local-color genre, but in the character of the heroine there is a marked departure from the sentimental heroine pattern which is generally dominant in Thompson's fiction. Briefly, her lover is a fugitive because of an unjust court decision, and he is killed by a detective who is trying to capture him. The dectective is badly wounded in the fight, and it falls the heroine's lot to nurse him. When it appears that he is going to recover, her grief drives her to take a butcher knife into his room with the intention of killing him. Happily, he has suffered a relapse, and she discovers that he is dead just as she poises the knife over his throat. The heroine's decision to commit murder is quite an innovation in genteel fiction, although the trick ending, which saves her from the act, is a good index to the strength of Thompson's basic commitment to the canons of that fiction.

The local-color strain naturally is not limited to the local-color stories; it is also important in the historical romances, where Creole and backwoods characters play a notable part. In *The King of Honey Island* Thompson attempted to investigate the New Orleans milieu and the Creole character somewhat in the manner of Cable, but with less success. His Creoles, where not drawn according to the canons of the sentimental tradition, generally appear as cartoon Frenchmen—volatile, shoulder-shrugging, gesticulating gallants. In some historical short stories written during the early 1890's for the *Ledger* and growing out of his researches for his school history of Louisiana, he came much closer to Cable's Creoles.[17] In *Alice of Old Vincennes* he worked with the backwoods American, the Creole of the Mississippi valley, and the Indian. By the very nature of historical romance, the local color in these novels and tales is a kind of tour de force, for the reason that he was working with secondhand materials; it is a basically different situation from that of the Cherokee hills stories or the Hoosier sketches. But in the other novels, which he called romances but which also have several affinities with Howellsian realism, he again made good use of the local color which he knew at firsthand: North Georgia, Savannah, Tallahassee, the Alabama hill country, Indiana, Mobile, and Bay St. Louis.

These novels were Thompson's most serious efforts at fiction.[18]

Although the story was always the most important thing to him, he nevertheless dealt earnestly with contemporary problems as he saw them: the sectional attitudes of the South, West, and North and the relations between these sections; the effect of the business ethic and the gospel of success on American society; the situation of the literary artist, especially the provincial, in a money-grabbing society; the rise of the critical spirit of realism in literature; the rise of science; and the rise of feminism.

The autobiographical *A Banker of Bankersville* reveals, as we have seen, a good deal about the personal conflicts and the social problems which the ex-Rebel, newly arrived from Georgia, probably had to face in Crawfordsville; but here it is of interest as a curious combination of realism and the sentimentalism against which Howells and his friends were protesting. In the development of one character Thompson even leaned toward determinism, showing that as much as he deplored the encroachment of science upon art, he was still susceptible to some of the scientific ideas that were floating around, so to speak, in the intellectual climate of his day.

The sentimentalism can be seen in the idealization of human nature and relationships. Female nature in particular he portrayed as being spirited, courageous, true, and sensitive—almost beyond belief. The heroine of *A Banker of Bankersville,* when she learns that a mob of townspeople may lynch a young speculator because his luck changed after they had almost forced money on him in their greed to get something for nothing, does not hesitate a moment in deciding to go harangue and disperse them. That she fails serves to bring her partially back into the realm of plausibility. And the hero, without any previous experience in oratory, through his love for this magnificent girl is able to deliver an impassioned oration that eclipses one just delivered by the most famous trial lawyer in the state. It is also revealed that this same young man, when he became disaffected with the southern cause while serving as a Confederate officer, had boldly ridden up to his commanding general, handed him a sum of money sufficient to pay for his horse and arms, dramatically announced that he was leaving the army, wheeled his horse, and escaped before pursuit could be organized.

Lawson, the young man of easy morals, is the deterministically developed character. Completely without conscience, but with enormous physical strength and courage, a monomania for money, and strong personal magnetism, he cuts a wide swath wherever he moves—a prototype in a small way of Dreiser's Frank Cowperwood. He comes from a family of swindlers and petty criminals; his father's sudden appearance after release from prison constitutes one of the factors in the young man's "change of luck." "He had come," said Thompson, "from a long line of men who had lived by their wits, lived by the chances of the times, who had preyed upon mankind in seasons of need and misfortune. With him to trust to luck was hereditary. . . ."[19]

The realistic elements are numerous. This book, in fact, is Thompson's closest approach to Howellsian realism. When handling minor characters who are not under the necessity of living up to the sentimental ideals of human nature and action, he achieved some vivid and convincing portrayals. Mrs. Nora O'Slaughtery, for instance, the "bright and comely widow" who keeps the boarding house for gentlemen, as well as a receptive state of mind for any proposals of matrimony, appears to be a genuine transcript from life. When the young lawyer advises her to marry at the earliest possible moment the gentleman to whom she has become engaged, so that she may be relieved of the expense of giving him free board during his fiancé status, her reaction is that of real flesh-and-blood:

> "That's me moind, that's me moind," she exclaimed, . . . "Not that I care how long I wait, at all, but thin ayconomy, Mister Milford, ayconomy demands a change in affairs altogither for I can't afford the ixpinsive luxury of kaypin' 'im a-boardin' on me an' git no—that is not have—I should say—" she got hopelessly entangled and at the same time blushed scarlet.[20]

Other excellent bits of realism are the conspiracy scene between Lawson and McGinnis, one of the local bankers; the auction of all the worldly goods of one Tom Curry, a bankrupt, who is advised by the loungers that he "orta had better luck"; the revival meeting of Mrs. Goodword, the female evangelist; and all of the activities of Miss Sarah Anna Crabb, the chinless, buck-toothed female reporter who cherishes hopeless dreams of breaking into the eastern literary circles. And of course we must not omit the Hoosier farmers, rough, blunt, shrewd and money-minded, and "the partners of their joys"—their worn and apathetic women-folk—trailing behind them.

It is in this book, too, that Thompson treats most fully the social problems of his time. Although the principal concern is ostensibly the love story, the action really revolves around the moral and social effects of the gospel of success in a small Indiana city. The overweening desire to get rich quick leads most of the inhabitants into such extended speculations in the commodity market and certain shady securities that, when the market turns, almost everyone is wiped out. The losers. in their rage and chagrin, seek to make a scapegoat of Lawson, the leader in the speculations and the broker for a number of the victims. When they surround the jail, he calmly appears on a balcony and reminds them that the town, through his generosity, has new church furniture and a spacious park and that many of them have good investments in real property and sound securities, made with the "tainted" money he won for them before his luck turned. To this there is no answer, for there is no one in the mob qualified to cast the first stone. Only the young southerner, Milford, despite being Lawson's law partner, has from moral scruples avoided Lawson's schemes, but even he has to admit that he has knowingly profited from his association with the speculator, for it is Lawson who has brought all the firm's business. There seems to be no person in the town who has not been stained in some way, directly or indirectly, by contact with Lawson and his money. The book ends with the sober warning that "ill-gotten wealth is the greatest menace a free government has to confront."[21]

Feminism is criticized in the persons of Mrs. Goodword, Miss Crabb, and to a lesser degree, Marion Wilton, the heroine. Mrs. Goodword's religion is quite accurately diagnosed as a lust for power; Miss Crabb, although presented with a good deal of sympathy, is plainly a square peg in a round hole, alternately pitiful and repellent because she is deluded as to her own capabilities; and Miss Wilton, after being pumped full of insidious ambition at an eastern female seminary, is willing to admit, after her experience with the lynch mob, that there is a certain basic, irrational, and efficient difference between men and women which feminist ambitions cannot obliterate. She is then suitable for marriage to Milford.

The situation of the provincial artist is dealt with in the careers of young Milford and Miss Crabb. Here Thompson developed the same ideas that appeared in his criticism, namely that eastern editors, because of their urban corruption, are prejudiced against

the western writer. In addition, the provincial writer must endure
the jocosities of his hard-headed and success-minded fellow towns-
men, sometimes in a helpful spirit, sometimes in malice. One local
newspaper suggests that Milford, in a trial for which he is special
prosecutor, quote some of his love-poetry to insure the prisoner's
collapse. " 'The colonel's poetry is warranted to be sugar-coated
death to all sensible people.' "[22] Another time a well-meaning
farmer friend advises him, " 'If I was you, Mr. Milford, I'll be dern
if I'd write any more of them little pomes. . . . 'Course the pomes
is all right 'nough, but the folks in these parts don't take up with
the idee of a grown man a-foolin' away his time at sech doin's.
. . . If I was you I'd get to Congress or I'd bust a swingletree.
'Tain't no use a foolin' away yer chances on them pomes. It's too
much like a woman's doin's.' "[23] On the whole, said Thompson, the
country town is usually proud of its poet—but in the same way
that it is proud of its five-legged calf. At the same time, "it is
obscurely ashamed of him, believing him to be a sort of fun-
bundle for the rest of the world."[24]

The question of realism versus romance gets a good deal of attention in this as in other novels; and again the ideas of the critical
essays are repeated.[25]

The sectional contrasts are best studied in his two earliest
novels, *A Tallahassee Girl* and *His Second Campaign*.[26] In both,
Thompson revealed himself as a partisan of the postbellum Union.
Both are a part of the literary discovery of the South by the North
after the Civil War, and they follow the usual pattern of a love
affair between a northern man and a southern girl, in the course of
which each learns about the manners and morals of the other's
section. In the earlier one, *A Tallahassee Girl,* the lady is won by
her southern suitor, possibly indicating that as yet the South is
not ready to be completely reconciled with the North; but in the
second story the triumphant suitor is a Chicagoan, and the young
lady, with a mild feeling of guilt at her disloyalty, finds the forward-
looking optimism, the energy, the open friendliness, and the general newness of life in the North and West preferable to the ways
of Savannah. But Thompson, although he was impatient with
southerners who tried to relive the old days instead of adapting
themselves to the new regime, a la Henry Grady, still nursed a
strong nostalgia for the Old South. He did not deny the strong
tendency to homicide in the southern character, nor the tendency

of the antebellum South to forbid as subversive any criticism of its institutions; but in spite of these faults, the Old South had his deepest admiration. In *His Second Campaign* he digressed to argue, "The medieval spirit, as it existed during the two hundred years of Provençal glory, when knighthood and love and song and honor, each and all, were superbly arrayed and arranged in spectacular order, was the spirit of the old South when slavery was in its prime. Jousts and tournaments took the form of social contests for superiority in all that made hospitality charming and virtue safe; and despite the stain of human bondage, the old regime was that of the purest and most lovable aristocracy the world has ever seen."[27] This *Gone With the Wind* vision of plantation life does not fit with the reality described by historians and points up again that Thompson was really an outsider to this life. That his fleeting glimpses of it in boyhood, remembered through a romantic haze, could be used as a basis for serious social criticism emphasizes, as well, the radically uncritical quality of his mind.

Possibly because he was an admirer of the New South, his romances of southern life are concerned incidentally with the industrial development that was going on during the 1870's and 1880's. His Chicago hero is a railroad lawyer traveling in the South for the purpose of promoting a new road. In *At Love's Extremes* the Birmingham steel industry is constantly in the background. In *Sweetheart Manette,* the L.&N. Railroad from Mobile to New Orleans is being promoted. It is significant, however, that the industrial elements are not the "romantic" elements. These belong to the antebellum culture.

It is also significant that a high proportion of his heroes in these novels are independently wealthy men who are gentlemen, scholars, and patrons of the arts, or if not wealthy, at least artistically inclined. However much Thompson may have admired the energy and the optimism of the American businessman, he was not quite ready to make him a hero-symbol. As his criticism of the cult of success implies, his values were those of a culture in which the artist and intellectual were men of importance. These heroes, too, are the Anglo-Saxon rather than the Gallic type.

His heroines, with one exception, are in the sentimental tradition: bright, lovable, pure, dutiful, self-effacing, and considerate of their inferiors. The one exception, Milly, the strangely beautiful cracker girl in *At Love's Extremes,* is another example of a deterministically developed character, although in her physical beauty she represents an exceptional rather than a normal product of her heredity and environment. But morally and mentally she is almost a cipher. Hers, said Thompson, "was not a nature capable of much expansion or improvement. A long line of mountain ancestors had fixed in her the hereditary simpleness, narrowness and mental barrenness of the Sandlapper."[28] The fact that he attached more importance here to heredity and less to environment than did the later writers who embraced determinism as philosophical doctrine probably reflects his own preoccupation with biological rather than social science.

Milly's entire emotional nature is compassed in her blind adoration of the Byronic hero, a wealthy young man who, for certain vague reasons, has withdrawn temporarily from society to a retreat in the mountains. There is a seduction, under unstated circumstances; in fact, it is never mentioned directly, being revealed to the reader by the mute reaction of the girl's father to a whispered communication from her mother after the young man has been gone for some time. He eventually returns and marries the girl but only because he has been prevented from marrying a woman of his own class, whom he really loves, by the return of her husband, long thought to be dead. Some contemporary critics were abashed by this dealing, furtive as it is, with "unholy" love and by the marriage across class boundaries. Whether or not Thompson intended these details as innovation or revolt against the conventions in fiction of his time and class, they appeared to be that. But his later highly conventional and conservative practice would suggest that he was looking for a picturesque, *outré* situation to liven up his romance rather than consciously attempting to widen the bounds of fiction.

The broad tendencies of these romances of southern and western life can be summarized in a few words if we omit the exceptional aspects just noted. In all of them the plot constitutes the principal interest of the book. Secondarily, Thompson was concerned with portraying the manners and institutions of the culture with which he was dealing. In one sense this puts the stories in the tradition of local color, but where the tendency in local color is to concentrate on low life or humble life, Thompson was more concerned with the upper classes. The lower classes—Negroes, crackers, farmers— are introduced only for comic relief. His method, like James's, was to reveal the southern culture through its impact on an outsider. But the resemblance is only superficial here, for, unlike James, he was little concerned with the deeper psychological effects of that impact. He was superficial in another way, too. The industrial development of the New South frequently appears as a background, but its function is limited to just that. It is nothing more than a kind of scenic backdrop against which the characters move; it is never really important as a force in the life portrayed. Finally, Thompson's prime concern was with the unusual rather than the commonplace in both character and situation: his heroines are paragons; his heroes are rich or talented or supremely courageous or widely traveled—sometimes all. When the commonplace enters, it is as a foil for the unusual.

Considering that Thompson's widest fame has always been as the author of *Alice of Old Vincennes,* it is a little ironic that his historical romances should constitute such a relatively small part of his literary output. Strictly speaking, he wrote only two: *Alice of Old Vincennes* and *The King of Honey Island.* A third, "The Lily of Rochon,"[29] might be considered in this group, but it is a much slighter effort than the other two. Even slighter are the short stories which he wrote for the *Ledger;* they appear to be apprentice work for the longer romances.

Both of the longer novels were direct outgrowths of the research that Thompson did for his two school histories, and the novels both reflect a thorough saturation with the material. *The King of Honey Island* is centered about the Battle of New Orleans, and *Alice of Old Vincennes* is centered about the capture of Fort Sackville, at Vincennes, by George Rogers Clark. In a way that has since become standard for the historical romance, Thompson made use of the wealth of authentic detail that can be found in history books; and in a manner that goes back at least to Scott he utilized famous or near-famous historical personages and their actions as points of orientation for the story. Such figures as Edward Livingston, General Pakenham, Governor Claiborne, Jean Laffite and John A. Murrel stalk through the Louisiana story; and General Jackson is one of the principal characters. For *Alice of Old Vincennes,* Thompson drew quite heavily on William H. English's *Conquest of the Territory Northwest of the River Ohio,*[30] and one can see Colonel Clark, Captain Bowman, Francis Vigo, the British General Hamilton—the "hair-buyer"—very much in the way that English described them. For both novels Thompson introduced a love story with fictitious characters as the main interest.[31]

In techniques and conventions, these novels differ little from the ones already discussed. If anything, the characterization of fictitious persons tends a little more toward the stereotypes of the sentimental tradition, except possibly for Alice. Young Fairfax in *The King of Honey Island,* when he learns that his love has fallen into the hands of the British, holds his clenched fist against his forehead, groans and staggers back as if struck by a bullet; but when the battle begins he fights like a tiger because he knows he is fighting for her. The same applies to Beverley, Alice's lover. In all his feats of derring-do, "he had his love with him," said Thompson, "and where Love is there can be no cowardice, no surrender."[32] Another example of sentimental convention is the British officer, Captain Farnsworth, who is given to drink and lechery before he sees Alice but is reformed through his love, albeit hopeless, for her. Alice's ability to inspire, in fact, is so great that the action reads at times almost like burlesque, as for instance when she sends Beverley back to the fort to make a hopeless stand against the British—two men against five hundred. When Beverley complains " 'What can two or three men do against an army?' " she replies, with a shining countenance, " 'Fight and die like men. . . . Be heroic!' " and she adds,

> "It is your country, your flag, not me, that you must think of now."
> She folded her arms and stood boldly erect.
> Never before, in all his life, had he felt such a rebuke. He gave her a straight, strong look in the eyes.
> "You are right, Alice," he cried, and rushed from the house to the fort.
> She held her rigid attitude for a little while after she heard him shut the front gate of the yard so forcibly that it broke in pieces, then she flung her arms wide, as if to clasp something, and ran to the door; but Beverley was out of sight.[33]

Alice's patriotic fervor, and concomitant tendency to perform violence on the enemies of her country, distinguish her from the traditional sentimental heroine. She shoots Captain Farnsworth with a horse pistol when he threatens the village priest, and she runs Lieutenant Barlow through with a rapier when he tries to arrest her foster-father, who has assaulted the British commander.

And before she gets her shot at Farnsworth she confides in one of the other village girls, to whom he had tried to make love one evening when he had been drinking, " 'If Captain Farnsworth ever offers to treat me as he did you, mark my words, I'll kill him—kill him, indeed I will! You ought to see me! . . . I wish he would try it. How I would love to shoot him to pieces, the hateful wretch! I wish he would.' "[34] This bloodthirst is certainly not in the sentimental tradition, but it is in accord with Thompson's increasing apology for violence in his later years, in connection with his belief in Manifest Destiny and the cult of the Anglo-Saxon— ideas which find their reflection in the novel and which perhaps account for some of its popularity.[35]

Another reflection of Anglo-Saxon superiority in both of his historical romances is the ascription of general irresponsibility to the Creoles. It is always the Anglo-Saxon who gets things done, although the Creoles may help if they feel like it. Whenever a forceful character appears among the Creoles, he turns out to be an Anglo-Saxon in disguise. This is the case in *The King of Honey Island* with M. Vernon and with Pierre Rameau, who are both revealed as Scots; and in *Alice of Old Vincennes* the heroine is finally identified as a member of the fine old Tarleton family of Virginia, in order to explain her having all the Anglo-Saxon virtues despite her Creole rearing and to make her eligible to mate with a Beverley of the Virginia Beverleys.

In the fiction dealt with up to this point certain qualities are pervasive. There is the generally sentimental characterization. There is a certain impatience with technical problems resulting often in implausible plot and implausible dialogue, especially where upper class characters are concerned. Conversely, the handling of humble characters who would be expected to speak in dialect is often remarkably good. There is a conscious emphasis on plot and action, at the expense of psychological and moral analysis; the subtleties of individual feelings and interpersonal relations are ignored; there is, finally, a constant tendency on the part of the author to ride his critical hobbies in his fiction—attacks on realism, defenses of romance and of "Americanism" are interjected in the stories.

One book, omitted thus far, deserves to stand by itself, not for its literary excellence but rather for its unique character: *A Fortnight of Folly* is a satire on the American literary scene; and although it reveals Thompson as sometimes more intent on winning than on being fair to his opponents, it also reveals his considerable gift for humor and imaginative satire. He lays about him with a will and only the romancers after his own pattern are spared.

The method is to assemble a group of impecunious *littérateurs* at a summer resort hotel in the Smoky Mountains. This "select group" is invited by the proprietor, a speculator named Gaslucky, as a promotional stunt for his new Hotel Helicon; Miss Sarah Anna Crabb is therefore included, and Howells' Bartley Hubbard and James's Henrietta Stackpole are invited for a weekend in order to insure some good publicity. Only one member of the party is not a writer, and he is, incognito, the publisher of most of the writers present.

Realists, of course, get the hardest and most specific thumping. Thompson makes Bartley Hubbard turn upon his creator when some member of the party comments that it was not very realistic of Howells to draw him as a married man when in fact he was a bachelor. " 'Realist!' laughed Hubbard, 'why he does not know enough about the actual world to be competent to purchase a family horse. He's a good fellow, good and true and kind-hearted, but what does he know about affairs? He doesn't even know how to flatter women!' "[36] Howells is also attacked as Arthur Selby, the writer who, in the words of an anonymous guest, is at the present time " 'monopolizing the field of American fiction. In fact I think he claims the earth.' " And when a rather naive young lady attempts a timid defense of Zola, she is rebuked by being compared to Selby: " 'Oh, you talk just as Arthur Selby writes in his critical papers. He's all the time trying to prove that fiction is truth and that truth is fiction. He lauds Zola's and Dostoieffsky's filthy novels to the skies; but in his own novels he's as prudish and Puritanish as if he had been born on Plymouth Rock instead of on an Illinois prairie.' "[37]

Where the game is smaller, the humor is better, for example in the case of the intellectual Boston female, Mrs. Nancy Jones Black, or Miss Amelia Lotus Nebeker, who writes and recites New Jersey dialect verse. Miss Nebeker's rendering of "The Jerseyman's Jew's Harp," with the aid of a stray cat who manages to get its tail under her heel, is in the best tradition of western humor and is the one really hilarious scene in the book. It closes with a comment that is good enough to have come from Mark Twain: "Still the reading served to kill a good deal of time, by a mangling process."[38] Mrs. Black is described as follows:

> She was president of the Woman's Antiquarian Club, of the Ladies' Greek Association, of the Sappho Patriotic Club, of the Newport Fashionable Near-Sighted Club for the study of Esoteric Transcendentalism, and it may not be catalogued how many more societies and clubs. She was a great poet who had never written any great poem, a great essayist whom publishers and editors avoided, whom critics regarded as below mediocrity, but of whom everybody stood in breathless awe, and she was an authority in many literary and philosophical fields of which she really knew absolutely nothing. She was a reformer and a person of influence who had made a large number of her kinsfolk famous as poets and novelists without any apparent relevancy between the fame and the literary work done. If your name were Jones and you could trace out your relationship to Mrs. Nancy Jones Black and could get Mrs. Nancy Jones Black interested in your behalf, you could write four novels a year with great profit ever afterward.

Something of her method and her attitude is revealed in the advice she gives little Miss Moyne, to whom she has taken a great liking. " 'Milton John Jones, my nephew, was at first bound that he wouldn't let Tom, my brother, advertise him; but he soon saw his way clear, I assure you, and now he publishes four serials at once. Be prudent, dear, be prudent.' "[39]

Dialect fiction comes in for its share of scorn also. Peck, the Boston critic, who surreptitiously verifies his literary judgments by reference to the *Revue des Deux Mondes,* grumbles that " 'American literature, its fiction I mean, is founded on dialect drivel and vulgar yawp. Look at our magazines; four-fifths of their short stories are full of negro talk, or cracker lingo, or mountain jibberish, or New England farm yawp, or Hoosier dialect. It is horribly humiliating. It actually makes foreigners think that we are a nation of green-horns.' "[40] But he is alone in his objections, for when a picturesque mountaineer appears on the scene, most of the guests go into a huddle and fill the air with exclamations:

> "What a delicious character!"
> "What precious dialect!"
> "How typically American!"
> "A veritable hero!"
> "How like Tolstoi's lovely Russians he is," observed Miss Fide-

lia Arkwright of Boston, a nearsighted maiden who did translations and who doted on virile literature.

"When I was in Russia, I visited Tolstoi and his shoeshop—" began [another young writer], but nobody appeared to hear him, so busy were all in making notes for a dialect story.[41]

Finally, there is an extended attack on the usual royalty agreements between publisher and writer, in essentially the same terms with which Thompson pursued the subject in his criticism.

Until the success of *Alice of Old Vincennes,* Thompson's reputation as a fiction writer was more regional than national. When *Hoosier Mosaics* appeared in 1875 the eastern magazines gave it little notice. The *Independent* saw some power in its descriptions of natural scenes and liked the humor; one reviewer simply announced that another Goth had come out of the West; but in Indiana "the book was read [all over the state] and Mr. Thompson was pointed out by his fellow-townsmen with great pride as a distinguished man."[42]

The first of the Round Robin novels, *A Tallahassee Girl,* was generally well received, although one critic pointed out quite accurately that Thompson, using materials with which a better writer might have done much, had done little in the way of psychological study. Mostly there was praise for the charm of the local description and predictions of better things to come from the anonymous writer.[43] Possibly for that reason Osgood was willing to try another of Thompson's novels the next year. If so, he must have been disappointed to read the reviews, for *His Second Campaign* got a much less favorable reception.[44] The improbability of the plot and the flatness of the characterization were the principal objections. The *Literary World* marked it off with the comment, "well-meant and harmless."

With *At Love's Extremes* Thompson recouped his reputation slightly.[45] Nearly all of the critics agreed that here was good storytelling, with pathos, insight into rustic character, and some very fine landscape description; but they were also alienated by his handling of illicit love. For the heroine, Milly, the wages of sin is a rich husband, and that was not an acceptable conclusion.

The other books, all received reviews very similar to those of the early books—rather short, complimentary, but always with a reservation or two, never enthusiastic, except for Jeanette Gilder's review of *Alice of Old Vincennes.*[46]

The sales of Thompson's books were never large until the appearance of *Alice of Old Vincennes*. *A Tallahassee Girl* was the most steadily popular and was still read in the vicinity of Tallahassee until about 1920.[47] But the sales of *Alice of Old Vincennes* were, for that time, remarkable. The original publisher was the Bowen-Merrill Company of Indianapolis, who kept it in print until 1928 and sold more than 200,000 copies; in 1904 Grosset and Dunlap made reprints from the original plates and kept the book in print until 1941. For them it sold "well over the 150,000 mark." In England it was issued by Cassel and Company, but sales figures are not available.[48] Advance copies of the book were available in September, 1900; reviews began to appear in October; and by December it was in sixth place on the *Bookman's* list of bestsellers, a list based on reports from retail book merchants. In January, 1901, it was in first place, remaining there through June, though it shared first place with Irving Bacheller's *Eben Holden* during February and March. In July it went to third place, in August to fifth, and then lost out completely.[49] Charles Frohman, attracted by the dramatic possibilities of the story, arranged with the Bowen-Merrill Company for the dramatic rights and engaged Edward E. Rose to write the stage version. The play, starring Virginia Harned, opened at the Euclid Avenue Theater in Cleveland the following October. According to Lewis C. Strang's account of the play, the dramatist was one of a group of stage managers who "made a specialty of dramatizing novels," and who would guarantee out of hand to dramatize anything from a census report to the latest edition of Noah Webster's dictionary." The resulting version of *Alice of Old Vincennes* bore little resemblance to the novel. It was a four-act melodrama depending mostly upon colorful uniforms, threatened virtue, and pistol shots for its effect, but it seems to have run for a full season.[50]

After the popularity of *Alice of Old Vincennes* put Thompson's name before the public, many of his old books were reissued and enjoyed a substantial sale. These included *The King of Honey Island*, *A Banker of Bankersville*, *Milly*, and *Sweetheart Manette*, the latter published by Lippincott & Co. by means of binding sheets from the 1894 magazine printing. At the time of Thompson's death, the manuscript of *Rosalynde's Lovers* was not complete; but it had evidently been contracted for by the Bowen-Merrill Company, for it was completed by an unknown hand and published in the fall.[51]

Considering the number of historical and critical studies of American literature written during the past fifty years, Thompson has received little attention as a fiction writer; more often he is mentioned as a critic of realism.[52] When discussed as a fiction writer he is usually given a passing mention as one of the school of historical romancers who flourished at the end of the century.[53]

This slight notice is essentially just. Certainly Thompson belongs among the minor figures. In no area of fiction was he either a pioneer or an extraordinary practitioner. In his Gothic romances he was following the well-defined and sensational patterns set out by the New York *Weekly* and *Ledger;* in his romances of contemporary life he was usually one among many who were exploiting the North's new realization of the exotic aspects of the South. In only one of these—*A Banker of Bankersville*—did he exhibit interests and techniques that seem to forecast a future development for him in the direction that American literature was moving. But he passed up his chance of distinction as an interpreter of the contemporary Indiana scene, probably because he could find no market for it, and he was, first and last, determined to make a living from his writing. In the bulk of his local-color work he clearly followed the lead of Harte and Eggleston, Longstreet and Johnston; with all his deftness in transcribing dialect, even with the affectionate nostalgia that marks his North Georgia stories, one always feels that his account of the humble life is condescending, superficial, mainly comic. When a writer regards his material as something less than serious, he cannot make great art of it.

As a writer of historical romance who achieved notable popular success Thompson was not in the van that did yeoman service in establishing the vogue—here Mary Catherwood's New France romances are most important—nor does his achievement in the form approach that of Weir Mitchell, Winston Churchill, or Mary Johnston. Even his popular success was not entirely his own doing. Had the Bowen-Merrill Company not suggested to him that he use the material for a novel, *Alice of Old Vincennes* would have been a play. On the whole, he seems to have been an energetic but impatient writer—impatient with the tougher problems of story structure, character analysis, impatient sometimes with the problems of dialogue. The resulting technique is impressionistic; he lay on in broad strokes and left the subtler details to the reader's imagination. His constant tendency to seek new fields was another symptom of this impatience, a tendency evident in his life as well as his writing. When the grass is always greener in some other pasture, a single plot never gets thoroughly grazed.

AFTERWORD

IN VIEWING MAURICE THOMPSON as a man of letters, one is first
struck by his remarkable range of interest and activity, then by
the remarkable energy and enthusiasm which carried him through
his diversified career and which is clearly reflected in his style.
Along with it, whether cause or effect, is a certain lack of discipline
and system. His reading, though wide, was unsystematic and often
superficial. (In this sense, he was not a well-educated man.) His
judgments were impressionistic and sometimes contradictory; his
critical theory was completely eclectic and confused by poorly defined terms. As a creative writer he was impatient with technical
problems and did not consistently have that infinite capacity for taking pains which distinguishes the first-rate artist. His own lack of this
quality may partially explain his inability to appreciate it in the
one writer of his own generation who was supremely endowed
with it, Henry James. Not to be ignored, of course, are the circumstances of his work. He was first and last a magazinist, writing
to sell, meeting deadlines, producing a forbidding volume of
work. In such circumstances it was not easy to take pains, and the
habits established probably carried over into his work outside the
magazines. Another limiting factor was emotional dependence. Even
more than most men, he needed the community's approval. He
could not accept criticism and would go to any length to justify
himself when criticized. Though he flourished on controversy,
he never espoused a minority position. Whatever the community
approved, he shouted loudly for. This need led to a parochial view

of the world, in this case a genteel midwestern view. No less important was the limiting influence of his upbringing. Though he did not cleave in later life to all the details of his parents' fundamentalist religious views, his thinking was always circumscribed by the authoritarian spirit of this early nurture.

To be candid, one must admit that Thompson's stature as a man of letters does not grow on closer acquaintance. Sensitive and sincere and of quick intelligence, he was nevertheless so hag ridden by a narrow and dogmatic view of the world that his tentative promise of artistic achievement was never fulfilled; and his critical position was already undermined by a broader world view than he knew, even as he was defending it. He is important, then, not as an original critic or artist, though some of his nature poems and local-color stories are as good as anything of their type produced in the period, but as a peculiarly fine representative of his time and place. His work may well be the *locus classicus* of the Genteel Tradition as it developed in the Midwest.

The usual tendency to regard the Genteel Tradition as homogeneous may obscure this point. Actually, at least four versions of it can be identified: the New England, the New York (or Middle States), the southern, and the midwestern. To differentiate these fully would be the province of another book, but some of the sources and qualities of the midwestern can be briefly pointed out. It is a combination of New England and frontier influences. The Yankee schoolmaster established the educational system of the Midwest, bringing with him a strong respect for tradition and an overwhelmingly moral approach to art. Onto this New England intellectual tradition was grafted the enthusiastic and evangelical religion of the frontier and the assertive parochialism of frontier manners and politics. The result was a complex of ideas and values not always internally consistent but nonetheless cherished by those elements of society that hungered after culture and respectability. In social intercourse that type of refinement and reticence which we have come to call Victorian was the rule. In religion, liberal Protestantism was the view. In politics, Manifest Destiny, nationalism, laissez faire, and Progress were the dogmas. In art, New England was revered as the fountainhead, but at the same time art was seen as the handmaiden of the new and truly American culture that was growing in the Midwest, reflecting favorably the "best" of the native manners, morals, and politics. Though New

England values were the starting point, wherever they conflicted with native values, they were sacrificed, particularly in the case of conflict between urban and small town values; for midwestern gentility was even more thoroughly agrarian than the eastern brand.

Realism as a literary movement was an unorganized and often inchoate attempt by a minority to enlarge, to ventilate (in the radical sense) this genteel world view. Thompson's attack on realism points up at once the contemporary confusion about the nature of realism and the peculiar qualities of the genteel midwestern opposition to it. His popularity and editorial support indicate that he spoke for the great majority of readers in his time and place in his objections to realism: that it was foreign, un-American, anarchistic; that it was untrue to the best American life; that it was immoral, "fleshly"; that it failed to set a high example by idealizing human nature; that it was pessimistic and offered no hope for the future; that it was agnostic, materialistic; that it was not art because it dealt only with the commonplace. In many of these objections Thompson was not entirely wrong if we understand and go along with his faiths, values, and definitions. Realism did have certain foreign roots, but it also had certain native ones; and certainly what anarchism there was in America was not, as Thompson believed, mainly the result of foreign realistic fiction. Realism was untrue to the "best" American life if by that we mean the ideals of social grace to which the respectable middle-class midwesterner subscribed. It was pessimistic if optimism means resolutely closing the eyes to everything but the pleasant aspects of life. It was not capable of lifting or reforming if reform is to be achieved only by closing one's eyes to life as it is and thinking of life as it ought to be. Its tendency was materialistic insofar as its method made use of the scientific device of accumulating details. But Thompson also used the terms "materialist" in regard to realism as roughly equivalent to "anti-Christian"; and of course this was quite untrue of most realists, and especially of the ones Thompson was accusing—Howells and Tolstoi. Finally, realism was not art if, by definition, art must deal with the "elevated," the exceptional aspects of experience. In the light of such confusion about definitions and unstated assumptions, it is no wonder that the contemporary controversy generated more heat than light.

To emphasize the peculiarly midwestern quality of Thompson's view may imply that it had little in common with the eastern.

Such was not the case, as his considerable popularity in the East indicated. But on the whole the eastern protest against realism came from a different level. While men like G. E. Woodberry at Columbia University, Henry Van Dyke at Princeton, W. C. Brownell and P. E. More worked much in the manner of Matthew Arnold on what we might call the academic level, basing their opposition on an urbane, intellectual, and well-informed attempt to understand and utilize the cultural heritage, Thompson worked on what might aptly be described as the Chautauqua level. He was no less sincere than the others—indeed he was perfervid—and his reverence for the cultural tradition was no less than theirs. But he lacked the intellectual discipline of the academicians; he depended on emotion and snap judgment, and sometimes, it must be admitted, his knowledge of the cultural tradition was inadequate or was warped by his overstrong commitment to the popular dogmas of the time, e.g., Manifest Destiny. Another difference lay in the audience which these critics spoke to, or perhaps spoke for. The academicians addressed a literate, relatively sophisticated group, secure in their social status and their culture. Thompson addressed an aspiring, fluid, but basically insecure group, a group whose interest in Thompson's brand of culture waned rapidly as the new century developed—a phenomenon best documented by the rapid decline of the Chautauqua movement in this period. For all of these reasons the critical work of the academicians, though now outmoded, remained a vital force much longer than did Thompson's.

Finally, his attack on realism reveals that if realism had its roots partly in the West, it also had some of its strongest opposition there, in the combination of frontier mores and transplanted eastern culture—the moral and political objections stemming from the one and the artistic objections from the other. The strength of this transplanted eastern culture can also be seen in the protest that eastern editors were unaware of "western" culture. The transplant had taken such firm root that to the residents of the "Boston of the West" and "Athens of Indiana" it appeared almost indigenous.

It is a rare man whose qualities will endear him both to his contemporaries and to posterity. Much less rare is the man whose elevation, like that of the weathercock, is enjoyed so long as he accurately indicates which way the wind blows. When out of patience with the democratic process we call this phenomenon the apotheosis of mediocrity. When our own candidate wins, we call it something else. But by whatever name, it describes Thompson's situation. His popularity, though great, was short-lived because the wind shifted so radically after the First World War.

NOTES

Notes to Chapter I

1 Maurice Thompson, "A Trencher Memory of Old Days," *Independent,* XLIX (September 9, 1897), 1162.

2 Thompson to William Malone Baskervill, March 19, 1887, in Baskervill Papers, Joint University Libraries, Nashville. This letter and two undated, signed holograph letters are the basis of Baskerville's account of Thompson in *Southern Writers: Biographical and Critical Studies,* (2 vols.; Nashville, 1897).

3 This and the volumes mentioned in Notes 4 and 7 are in the remnant of Maurice Thompson's library and personal papers collected by his late granddaughter, Josephine Ballard Davis, and now in the Emory University Library. Referred to hereinafter as the Davis Collection.

4 *The Autobiography of Elder Wilson Thompson; Embracing a Sketch of His Life, Travels, and Ministerial Labors, in Which is Included a Concise History of the Old Order of Regular Baptist Churches,* edited by his children (Cincinnati, 1873).

5 One of the governors was David Wallace, father of the flamboyant Lew Wallace, who was later to become one of Maurice Thompson's closest friends.

6 Thompson, "A Christian Silhouet [*sic*] of 1812," *Independent,* XLVI (June 21, 1894), 786.

7 Wilson Thompson, *Simple Truth: Illustrated in Eight Short Discourses on the System of Salvation by Jesus Christ; As Revealed in the Sacred Scriptures* (Lebanon, Ohio, 1821); Wilson Thompson, *The Triumphs of Truth or The Scripture a Sure Guide to Zion's Pilgrims* (Lebanon, Ohio, 1825).

8 Thompson to Baskervill, undated letter in Baskervill Papers. The Davis Collection includes his grandfather's books, but none by his father. I could discover none elsewhere.

9 Thompson, in his letter of March 19, 1887, to Baskervill gives September 7 as his birth date. All other sources give September 9, including a holograph note by Thompson, discovered by R. E. Banta, tipped into a volume in the Wabash College Library. Thompson dropped the "James" about 1875.

10   *Book News,* X (April, 1892), 349; Thompson, "In Sherman's Path," MS in Davis Collection.

11   Thompson to Baskervill, undated letter in Baskervill Papers.

12   Thompson, *By-Ways and Bird Notes* (New York, 1885), 101.

13   Thompson to Baskervill, undated letter in Baskervill Papers.

14   Thompson, "Longfellow—Flower de Luce," *Scott's,* IV (July, 1867), 491.

15   Thompson, "A Forest Beauty," *Lippincott's,* XXXVI (August, 1885), 200.

16   Thompson, "The Heresy of the Gad," *Independent,* XLIX (April 8, 1897), 431.

17   Thompson, "A Trencher Memory of Old Days," 1162.

18   *Ibid.*

19   Thompson, *By-Ways and Bird Notes,* 118-19.

20   Thompson, "The School in the Woods," *St. Nicholas,* VI (October, 1879), 837.

21   "Maurice Thompson," *Literary News,* VII (July, 1886), 220.

22   Thompson, "A Siren's Whisper," *Independent,* XLVII (February 28, 1895), 263.

23   Thompson to Baskervill, undated letter in Baskervill Papers.

24   Thompson, *By-Ways and Bird Notes,* 118-32; Thompson to Baskervill, undated letter in Baskervill Papers.

25   Thompson, "Genius and Enthusiasm," *Independent,* XXXIX (March 17, 1887), 326.

26   Thompson, "Halcyon Notes," *Independent,* XLI (February 28, 1889), 261; Thompson, "James Russell Lowell," *Critic,* XIV (February 23, 1889), 86.

27   Thompson, "Some Notes on Southern Literature," *Independent,* XXXVI (February 21, 1884), 226.

28   Thompson, "Footnotes for an Old-Time Southern Book," *Independent,* XLIX (July 15, 1897), 897.

29   Thompson to Baskervill, undated letter in Baskervill Papers.

30   Thompson, *Sylvan Secrets* (New York, 1887), 67.

31   Thompson to Baskervill, undated letter in Baskervill Papers.

32   Thompson, "Bow Shooting," *Scribner's,* XIV (July, 1877), 273.

33   Thompson, "The School in the Woods," 837.

34   Thompson, "Bow Shooting," 273.

35   Thompson, "The School in the Woods," 838.

36   Thompson, "Geology as a Summer Pastime," *Independent,* XLVIII (August 13, 1896), 1093.

37   Thompson to Baskervill, undated letter in Baskervill Papers.

38   Thompson, "Footnotes for an Old Time Southern Book," 897.

39   Thompson, *Stories of the Cherokee Hills* (Boston, 1898), 2-3. "Still-house meets" were convivial gatherings for the purpose of sampling the product of the local distillers.

40   Jessie Thompson Ballard, "Pioneer Georgia Preacher," Atlanta *Journal,* February 4, 1934, p. 9.

41   Thompson, "A Christian Silhouet of 1812," 786.

42   Walter Blair, Theodore Hornberger, and Randall Stewart (eds.), *The Literature of the United States* (Rev. ed.; 2 vols.; New York, 1953), II, 276.

43   Work Projects Administration, *Georgia: A Guide to its Towns and Countryside* in "American Guide Series" (Athens, Ga., 1940), 59.

44   Thompson to Baskervill, undated letter in Baskervill Papers.

45   Thompson, "In Sherman's Path."

46   Thompson to Gilder, December 17, 1894, in Century Collection, New York Public Library; Thompson, "The Ballad of a Little Fun," *Century,* L (June, 1895), 306-307.

47 Thompson, "A Siren's Whisper," 263.

48 Thompson, *Stories of the Cherokee Hills,* 4.

49 Parole Pass, May 12, 1865, in Davis Collection.

50 Thompson, *The Witchery of Archery* (Pinehurst, N.C., 1928), 233. An earlier edition of this book, published in 1878, is cited elsewhere.

51 Clement A. Evans (ed.), *Confederate Military History,* (12 vols.; Atlanta, 1899), VI, 131, 205, 301, 304-308.

52 Lulie Pitts, *History of Gordon Couty, Georgia* (Calhoun, Ga., 1933), 142.

53 *The War of the Rebellion: A Compilation of the Official Records of the Union and Confederate Armies* (73 vols.; Washington, D.C., 1880-1901), Ser. I, Vol. XXXIX, Pt. 3, p. 382, and Vol. XLIX, Pt. 1, pp. 508-509. Hereinafter cited as *Official Records* (unless otherwise indicated, all citations are to Series I).

54 T. Conn Bryan, *Confederate Georgia* (Athens, Ga., 1953), 154.

55 *Ibid.,* 154-55.

56 Thompson, to Paul Hamilton Hayne, February 1, 1876, in Hayne Collection, Duke University Library.

57 G. W. Coleman, Jr. "The Homes of Some Southern Authors," *Chautauquan,* VIII (March, 1888), 344.

58 Thompson, "The Court of Judge Lynch," *Lippincott's,* LXIV (August, 1899), 254.

59 Frank L. Mott, *A History of American Mazagines* (3 vols.; Cambridge, 1938), III, 46.

60 James W. Davidson, *Living Writers of the South* (New York, 1869), 558.

61 Thompson to Baskervill, undated letter in Baskervill Papers.

62 Pitts, *History of Gordon County,* 458.

63 Thompson, "Bow Shooting," 273.

64 Thompson, *The Witchery of Archery* (New York, 1878), 104.

65 Thompson, *The Witchery of Archery* (1928), 233.

66 Thompson, "Three Weeks of Savage Life," *Appleton's,* XIV (September 4, 1875), 303.

67 *Book News,* X (April, 1892), 349; Thompson to Baskervill, undated letter in Baskervill Papers.

68 "The Late Maurice Thompson," *Bookman,* XII (April, 1901), 110. In *Hoosier Mosaics* (New York, 1875) Thompson said that Colfax, Indiana, was the junction of the L.C.&S.W. and the I.C.&L. For other information in the foregoing pages pertaining to the town, John Lee, and the railroads, I draw variously on R. E. Banta (ed.), *Indiana Authors and Their Books* (Crawfordsville, 1949); on Writers' Program, *Indiana: A Guide to the Hoosier State* ("American Guide Series" [New York, 1941]), 350-52; on Irving McKee *"Ben Hur" Wallace* (Berkeley, 1947); on letters to me from Mrs. Anita Lee Washburn of Indianapolis, granddaughter of John Lee; and on conversations with Miss Edith M. Coons, R. E. Banta, Walter B. Remley, and Professor James I. Osborne, all of Crawfordsville.

69 Thompson to Baskervill, undated letter in Baskervill Papers.

70 Thompson, *Scott's* (September, 1868) V, 660.

71 Thompson to Baskervill, undated letter in Baskervill Papers.

72 Thompson, *A Banker of Bankersville* (New York, 1886), 122.

73 Thompson to R. W. Gilder, October 25, 1886, in Century Collection.

74 McKee, *"Ben Hur" Wallace,* 122.

75 Thompson, "Merry Days with Bow and Quiver," *Scribner's,* XVI (May, 1878), 1-15; Thompson, "The Haunts of the Grayling," *Lippincott's* XXVIII (September, 1881), 268.

76 Thompson to William Dean Howells, June 2, 1881, in Howells Papers, Houghton Library, Harvard University.
77 Mary Hannah Krout, "Maurice Thompson at Home," *Independent*, LIII (February 21, 1901), 416.
78 Thompson to Hayne, November 15, 1875, in Hayne Collection.
79 Thompson to Hayne, October 20, 1876, in Hayne Collection.
80 Thompson to R. W. Gilder, October 25, 1886, in Century Collection.
81 Thompson to Baskervill, undated letter in Baskervill Papers.
82 Indianapolis *Journal*, September 19, 1889.
83 Frank H. Ristine, "Maurice Thompson," *Dictionary of American Biography* (22 vols.; New York, 1928-58), XVIII, 160-61. The sketches have not been identified.
84 This and subsequent tabulations of Thompson's work are based on Dorothy R. Russo and Thelma L. Sullivan, *Bibliographical Studies of Seven Authors of Crawfordsville, Indiana* (Indianapolis, 1952), 171-283.
85 Thompson to Hayne, December 8, 1876, and February 16, 1875, in Hayne Collection. The novel was eventually serialized as "Summer Sweethearts" in *Outing*, January-July, 1884, after an unsuccessful attempt to sell it to Osgood. See Thompson to Osgood, September 4, 1883, in Benjamin Holt Ticknor Papers, Manuscript Division, Library of Congress.
86 Thompson to Hayne, July 16, 1874, and February 1, 1876, in Hayne Collection.
87 Thompson to Baskervill, undated letter in Baskervill Papers.
88 Thompson, *A Banker of Bankersville*, 26.
89 Thompson to Howells, September 7, 1881, in Howells Papers.
90 Thompson to Howells, May 20, 1881, in Howells Papers.
91 Thompson to Hayne, March 29, 1881, in Hayne Collection.
92 Thompson to Howells, May 20, 1881, in Howells Papers.
93 Thompson to Howells, June 2, 1881, June 9, 1881, in Howells Papers.
94 Howells, "Maurice Thompson and His Poems," *Independent*, XXXV (October 4, 1883), 1249.
95 Thompson to Hayne, March 27, 1882, in Hayne Collection. Thompson wrote that Will had "moved away." Will Thompson eventually became general counsel for the Great Northern Railroad in Seattle.
96 Thompson, "Summer Recreation," *Independent*, XLVIII (June 4, 1896), 743.
97 Krout, "Maurice Thompson at Home," 416.
98 Thompson, *My Winter Garden* (New York, 1900), vii.
99 Thompson, "A Winter Retreat for Writers," *America*, IV (August 28, 1890), 610.
100 Russo and Sullivan, *Bibliographical Studies*, 244. For a full account of the organization, see L. May Wheeler and Mary E. Cardwell, *The Western Association of Writers: A Souvenir of the Fourth Annual Convention* (Richmond, Ind., 1890).
101 "The Lounger," *Critic*, IX (October 16, 1886), 187.
102 Charles Forster Smith, *Reminiscences and Sketches* (Nashville, 1908), 124.
103 Thompson to R. W. Gilder, April 6, 1888, in Century Collection. See also Nashville *Daily American*, April 5, 7, 1888.
104 Thompson's letter of thanks to Moses Coit Tyler dated September 26, 1887, is in the Cornell University Library.
105 Thompson to R. W. Gilder, November 26, 1888, in Century Collection.
106 *Critic*, XI (February 23, 1889), 85,
107 Quoted in *ibid.*, March 9, 1889, 124.
108 *America*, II (July 4, 1889), 438.

109 "Mr. Maurice Thompson Becomes an Editor of the INDEPENDENT," *Independent*, XLI (October 3, 1889), 1274.
110 P. E. More, "Books and Literature," *Independent*, LXV (December 10, 1908), 1420.
111 Thompson to R. W. Gilder, November 26, 1888, in Century Collection.
112 *Critic*, XIII (December 15, 1888), 307.
113 Thompson to R. W. Gilder, October 25, 1886, in Century Collection. The story was "Hodson's Hide-out."
114 Thompson to Gilder, June 4, 1886, in Century Collection.
115 Thompson to Gilder, November 25, 1886, in Century Collection.
116 Thompson to Gilder, October 25, 1886, in Century Collection.
117 Thompson to Gilder, November 25, 1886, in Century Collection.
118 Thompson to Gilder, April 6, 1888, in Century Collection.
119 Thompson to Gilder, undated letter (written between April 6 and April 18, 1888, from its relation to letters of those dates) in Century Collection.
120 William Hayes Ward, "Sixty Years of the INDEPENDENT," *Independent*, LXV (December 10, 1908), 1345.
121 Poetry: *Poems* (Boston, 1892); *Lincoln's Grave* (Cambridge and Chicago, 1894). Novels: *The King of Honey Island* (New York, 1893); *The Ocala Boy* (Boston, 1895); *Alice of Old Vincennes* (Indianapolis, 1900); *Sweetheart Manette* (Philadelphia, 1901), first published in *Lippincott's*, 1894. Stories: *Stories of the Cherokee Hills* (Boston, 1898). Essays: *The Ethics of Literary Art* (Hartford, 1893); *My Winter Garden* (New York, 1900). History: *Stories of Indiana* (Chicago, 1898). The manuscript novel was *Rosalynde's Lovers*, later published (Indianapolis, 1901). The manuscript volumes of nature essays, now in the Davis Collection, are "Toxophilus in Arcadia" and "With Bow and Rod."
122 Stedman to Thompson, September 22 and December 1, 1892, in Columbia University Library.
123 *Independent*, XLIII (June 4, 1891), 842.
124 *Ibid.*, XLV (July 13, 1893), 937.
125 Thompson to Candler, February 15, 1898, Emory University Library. See also unidentified newspaper clipping from a Pittsburgh paper in Davis Collection.
126 Russo and Sullivan, *Bibliographical Studies*, 262n.
127 The earliest letter Thompson wrote from Sherwood Place, dated April 26, 1893, is to Joseph B. Gilder, editor of the *Critic* and is in the New York Public Library.
128 Thompson to Joseph B. Gilder, April 30, 1896; in New York Public Library.
129 Thompson to Joseph B. Gilder, April 26, 1893, in New York Public Library.
130 In addition to the sources mentioned in Notes 5, 10, 21, 57, 61, 69, and 84, useful biographical studies are to be found in the following: Indianapolis *News*, February 15, 1901; New York *Times*, February 16, 1901; *Current Literature*, XXX (April, 1901), 490; *Critic*, XXXVIII (March, 1901), 212; *ibid.* (April, 1901), 292; *Literary News*, XXII (April, 1901), 111; *Literary World*, XVI (July 25, 1885), 259; *Independent*, LIII (February 21, 1901), 452-53; *Who's Who in America*, 1898; *National Cyclopedia of American Biography* (New York, 1909); Mildred Rutherford, *American Authors* (Atlanta, 1894).

Notes to Chapter II

1 Indianapolis *News*, February 15, 1901.
2 *Independent*, LIII (June 6, 1901), 1285.
3 Krout, "Maurice Thompson at Home," 416.

4   See Henry C. Tracy, *American Naturists* (New York, 1930), pp. 130-37;
    Lucille W. Wilkenson, "James Maurice Thompson, Nature-Poet," *Nature
    Study,* XIX (November, 1923), 361-66; Howard Zahniser, "In September,"
    Nature Magazine, XXVIII (September, 1936), 135.

5   Thompson, "A Forest Beauty," 200.

6   Thompson, "Three Weeks of Savage Life," in *The Witchery of Archery*
    (1878). In the original version, published in *Appleton's* XIV (September
    4, 1875), 303-10, the trader's remark does not appear; the piece is a pure
    idyl. This might indicate that the appeal of savage life had lessened
    slightly in the intervening years.

7   Thompson, *By-Ways and Bird Notes,* 117.

8   *Ibid.,* 73. See also Thompson, "Idle Day," *Independent,* LII (May 3, 1901),
    1053; Thompson, "A Leaf from a Fly-Book," *Independent,* XLVIII (April
    18, 1895), 509.

9   Thompson, "Beside Running Water," *Independent,* XLVI (April 18, 1894),
    485.

10 Thompson, "A Leaf from a Fly-Book," 509.

11 Thompson, *A Touch of Nature* (Cincinnati, 1906), 19.

12 Thompson, "The Bird of Optimism," *Independent,* XLVIII (June 16,
    1896), 75. ·

13 Thompson, "A Leaf from a Fly-Book," 509.

14 Thompson, "Sketching for Literary Purposes," *Critic,* IV (January 26,
    1884), 37.

15 Thompson, *Sylvan Secrets,* 70; Thompson, "Swamp Notes," *Critic,* IX
    (April 17, 1886), 196.

16 Thompson, *Sylvan Secrets,* 70; Thompson, *My Winter Garden,* 90.

17 Thompson, *My Winter Garden,* 116; Thompson, *Sylvan Secrets,* 82. In this
    ascription of personality to birds he may be a forerunner of the Ernest
    Thompson Seton school of animal biographers.

18 Thompson, *Sylvan Secrets,* 15.

19 Thompson, *By-Ways and Bird Notes,* 33-34.

20 Thompson, "The Faculty of Flight," *Independent,* LII (March 15, 1900),
    663.

21 Thompson, *By-Ways and Bird Notes,* 163.

22 Thompson, *Sylvan Secrets,* 6.

23 *Ibid.,* 6-7.

24 *Ibid.,* 9.

25 *Ibid.,* 8. One would like definitions here of "fact" and "prove."

26 Thompson, "Archer in the Cherokee Hills," *Atlantic,* LXXIX (April,
    1897), 472.

27 Thompson, *Sylvan Secrets,* 10.

28 Thompson, *By-Ways and Bird Notes,* 75-94.

29 *Ibid.,* 178-79.

30 Thompson, "The Sap-Sucker," *Appleton's,* VIII (December 7, 1872), 631.

31 Thompson, "The Haunts of the Grayling," 268-72; Thompson, "Grand
    Traverse Bay," *Lippincott's,* XXVIII (October, 1881), 321-33.

32 Thompson, *By-Ways and Bird Notes,* 39; Thompson, 196.

33 Thompson, "Confessions of an Ancient Poacher," *Outing,* XXXVII (No-
    vember, 1900), 134-38.

34 Indianapolis *News,* February 15, 1901.

35 McKee, *"Ben Hur" Wallace,* 247.

36 Thompson, "The Anatomy of Bird Song," in *Sylvan Secrets,* 101-23; I am
    also indebted to conversations with Dr. W. J. Breckenridge, curator of the
    University of Minnesota Museum of Natural History.

37 Review of Thompson's *My Winter Garden,* in *Dial,* XIII (July 16, 1901), 57.

38 See comments of Dr. A. W. Brayton in the Indianapolis *News,* February 15, 1901.

39 Robert P. Elmer, *Archery* (Philadelphia, 1926), Chap. 3.

40 Thompson, "On the Prairie's Edge," *Independent,* LI (October 19, 1889), 2801.

41 Thompson, *My Winter Garden,* 116-39.

42 *Ibid.,* 149-61.

43 An enterprising publisher apparently noted his kinship with Lamb in 1893, when the International Book Co. (New York) reprinted *Sylvan Secrets* and *Essays of Elia* in one volume.

44 This trait also appears in his fiction and its significance is discussed in Chap. 5.

45 Thompson, *The Witchery of Archery* (1878), 34.

46 *Ibid.,* 75-76.

47 It does not achieve the dramatic intensity of "The Vision of Sudden Death," but it approaches it by the same method. The Poe affinity is more vague—a matter of atmosphere devices: darkness, water, isolation.

48 Thompson, *By-Ways and Bird Notes,* 92.

49 Howells, "Recent Literature," *Atlantic,* XLIV (August, 1879), 269.

50 *Harper's,* LVII (October, 1878), 785; *Lippincott's,* XXII (October, 1878), 518; *Literary World,* IX (October, 1878), 74; *Nation,* XXVII (September 26, 1878), 200; *Scribner's,* XVI (September, 1878), 754.

51 *Critic,* VII (September 26, 1885), 147.

52 *Atlantic,* LVI (November, 1885), 720.

53 *Literary World,* XVI (November 14, 1885), 403.

54 *Critic,* XIV (February 16, 1889), 75.

55 *Nation,* LXXI (November 22, 1900), 406; *Dial,* XXXI (July 16, 1901), 57.

56 *Independent,* LII (December 13, 1900), 2997.

57 Thompson, "The Fletcher's Art," *Independent,* XLVII (July 25, 1895), 986.

58 Ethelbert D. Warfield, "Bird-Life in Recent Literature," *Southern Bivouac,* II (November, 1886), 368-71.

59 "Maurice Thompson," *Book News,* X (April, 1892), 349.

60 See especially "Story of Maurice Thompson's Life and Work," Indianapolis *News,* February 15, 1901; Lew Wallace's tribute, *ibid.;* Lloyd Mifflin, "Nature," *Independent,* LIII (March 7, 1901), 529; Thompson, "Rocked in the Wind's Cradle," *Independent,* LIII (June 6, 1901), 1285.

61 Riley's poem appears in the issue of the Indianapolis *News* cited in Note 60. Riley's mention of the escape element in Thompson's attitude toward nature is the first and only mention of it so far as I know among Thompson's critics. Lloyd Mifflin was a Pennsylvania poet who shared Thompson's enthusiasm for Greek pastoral poetry. His tribute appeared in the issue of the *Independent* cited in Note 60.

62 Frank Norris, "The 'Nature' Revival in Literature," in *The Responsibilities of the Novelist* (Garden City, 1928), 106-108.

63 See Note 4.

64 *Atlantic,* XLIV (October, 1879), 548.

Notes to Chapter III

1 Thompson, "A Leaf from a Fly-Book," 509; Thompson, *The Ethics of Literary Art,* 6, 47.

2 Thompson, *The Ethics of Literary Art,* 54; Thompson, "Art and Responsibility," *Independent,* XLII (November 27, 1890), 1667.

3 Thompson, *Sylvan Secrets*, 26-35.

4 Thompson, "Poe and Baudelaire: The Question of Their Sanity," *Independent*, XXVIII (January 27, 1876), 3. In reading this essay it is hard to escape the impression that Thompson did not know the facts about the deaths of Keats, Shelley, and Byron. It is equally hard to believe that he would write such an essay for publication without trying to ascertain the facts.

5 Thompson, "Cleanliness and Sanity," *Independent*, XLIV (February 4, 1892), 150.

6 Thompson, "Novels and Morals," *Independent*, XLIX (November 18, 1897), 1486; Thompson, "The Nude in Fiction," *America*, VI (June 18, 1891), 330.

7 Thompson, "Genius and Enthusiasm," 326.

8 Thompson, "Geology as a Summer Pastime," 1093.

9 Thompson, "Literary Perfume," *Critic*, XI (August 13, 1887), 73.

10 Thompson, "The Romance and the Novel," *Chautauquan*, XVI (October, 1892), 42.

11 Thompson, "Sketching for Literary Purposes," 37.

12 Thompson, "The Touch of Magic," *Independent*, L (November 3, 1898), 1257.

13 Thompson, "The Source of Originality," *Independent*, LI (February 2, 1899), 331. He also equates freshness and the picturesque. See Thompson, "The Picturesque in Poetry," *Independent*, XXXVII (February 12, 1885), 194.

14 Thompson, "The Touch of Magic," 1257.

15 Thompson, "The Melic Charm," *Independent*, XLVI (January 4, 1894), 3.

16 Thompson, "Food for the Gods," *Critic*, XXVII (April 11, 1896), 249.

17 Thompson, "The Pierian Freshness," *Independent*, XLV (January 19, 1893), 71.

18 Thompson, *The Ethics of Literary Art*, 83.

19 Thompson, "Scattered Stitches," *Independent*, XLIII (December 17, 1891), 1868.

20 Thompson, "Fame and Popularity," *Independent*, XLIX (June 24, 1897), 804. This doctrine of the immanent taste of the elect has a noteworthy resemblance to the Calvinist and Primitive Baptist doctrines of the divine election and the perseverance of the saints.

21 Thompson, "Alienism and Patriotism," *America*, I (April 21, 1888), 1; Thompson, "The Limit of Criticism," *Independent*, XLII (March 6, 1890), 305; Thompson, "The New Influence of Religious Journals," *Independent*, XLIII (February 26, 1891), 289.

22 Thompson, *The Ethics of Literary Art*, 35-36; Thompson, "Realistic Christianity," *Independent*, XXXIX (October 13, 1887), 1293.

23 Thompson to R. W. Gilder, August 30, 1889, in Century Collection.

24 Thompson, "The Alien Taint in Criticism," *America*, II (August 15, 1889), 631.

25 Thompson, "The Limit of Criticism," 305; Thompson, "The Critics and the Russian Novels," *Independent*, XXXVIII (September 16, 1886), 1163; Thompson, *The Ethics of Literary Art*, 24.

26 Thompson, "Cant and Criticism," *Independent*, XL (May 24, 1888), 642.

27 Thompson, "The Low Tide in Poetry," *America*, V (February 12, 1891), 564; Thompson, "Urban Censorship," *Independent*, XLIII (May 21, 1891), 739; Thompson, "Criticism by the Rule of Darwin," *Independent*, L (December 8, 1898), 1697.

28 Thompson, "Imaginative Romance," *Scott's*, IV (December, 1867), 924.

29 Thompson, "The Domain of Romance," *Forum*, VIII (November, 1889), 329; Thompson, "The Alien Taint in Criticism," 631; Thompson, "Balzac, Sainte-Beuve, and the Realists," *America*, II (July 11, 1889), 470.

30 Thompson, "The Return of Romance," *Independent*, L (December 15, 1898), 1735.

31 Thompson, "The Alien Taint in Criticism," 631.

32 Thompson, "Heroes and Heroines in Fiction," *America*, V (January 15, 1891), 454; Thompson, "Budding Poets," *Independent*, XLVII (January 24, 1895), 104; Thompson, "Browning as a Poet," *America*, III (January 2, 1890), 439; Thompson, *The Ethics of Literary Art*, 59-60.

33 His criticism of financial speculation in *A Banker of Bankersville* (See Chap. 5) is consistent with the values of this society, whose attitude on this question might be stated thus: business is business but gambling is gambling.

34 Thompson, *The Ethics of Literary Art*, 70-71. See also Thompson, "The Lesson of Fiction," *Independent*, L (September 15, 1898), 763.

35 Thompson, "The Theory of Fiction-Making," *Chautauquan*, XIV (October, 1891), 46.

36 Thompson, *The Ethics of Literary Art*, 65 ff.

37 Thompson, "The Turning of the Tide," *Independent*, XLVIII (February 20, 1896), 238; Thompson, "Balzac's Romances," *Independent*, XLVII (November 21, 1895), 1565.

38 Thompson, "The Critics and the Romancers," *Independent*, LII (August 9, 1900), 1919. The terms and the mode of distinction are derived from James Lane Allen's "Two Principles in Recent American Fiction," *Atlantic*, LXXX (October, 1897), 433.

39 Thompson, "The Theory of Fiction-Making," 46; Thompson, "The Novels That Shakespeare Read," *America*, IV (July 31, 1890), 498.

40 Thompson, "The Analysts Analyzed," *Critic*, IX (July 10, 1886), 19; Thompson, "Cant and Criticism," 642.

41 Thompson, "Fiction and Moral Lessons," *Independent*, XLVI (August 30, 1894), 1112; Thompson, "Cant and Criticism," 642; Thompson, "Passion in Poetry and Fiction," *Independent*, XXXIX (June 30, 1887), 806.

42 Thompson, "The Western Literary Outlook," *Chautauquan*, VII (February, 1887), 277.

43 Thompson, "How to Study Literature," *Chautauquan*, XVIII (November, 1893), 147; Thompson, "The Sapphic Secret: Rejoinder to John Burroughs," *Critic*, XXIV (March 31, 1894), 211.

44 Thompson, "Materialism and Criticism," *America*, III (November 7, 1889), 183.

45 Thompson, "Materialism and Criticism," 183; Thompson, "The Domain of Romance," 329; Thompson, "Handicapped Critics," *Independent*, XXXIX (February 3, 1887), 134. This accusation of photography was palpably unfair to American realists, but it was a common one and was justified to a degree by their defense of Zola's *Experimental Novel*.

46 Thompson, "The Analysts Analyzed," 19; Thompson, "Literary Perfume," 73.

47 Thompson, "The Analysts Analyzed," 19.

48 Thompson, "Concerning Enthusiasm," *Independent*, XXXVII (September 24, 1885), 1223; Thompson, "Will Imagination Run Dry?" *Cosmopolitan*, XXVIII (April, 1900), 623; Thompson, "The Analysts Analyzed," 19; Thompson, "The Touch of Genius," *America*, III (December 26, 1889),

407; Thompson, "Studies of Prominent Novelists, No. 4: Thomas Hardy," *Book News,* VI (January, 1888), 223; Thompson, "Science and Inspiration," *Independent,* XLI (December 26, 1889), 1719.

49 Thompson, "The Analysts Analyzed," 19; Thompson, "The Tendency of Art in Fiction," *Independent,* XXXVI (October 9, 1884), 1281.

50 Thompson, "The Analysts Analyzed," 19; Thompson, "Alienism and Patriotism," 1; Thompson, "The Literary Lesson of Anarchy," *Independent,* XXXIX (December 8, 1887), 1574.

51 Thompson, "Women in Novels," *America,* II (September 5, 1889), 727; Thompson, "A Bit of Realism," *Independent,* XLV (November 16, 1893), 1534.

52 Thompson, "The Critics and the Romancers," 1919.

53 Thompson, "The Test of Originality," *Independent,* XLV (October 12, 1893), 1361.

54 Thompson, "A Hint to Critics," *Independent,* XLII (July 10, 1890), 951; Thompson, "The Touch of Inspiration," *Independent,* XLIII (February 5, 1891), 187.

55 Thompson, "The Pierian Freshness," 71.

56 Thompson, "The Basis of Art," *America,* IV (April 24, 1890), 103.

57 Thompson, "To Return to Nature," *Independent,* XLIX (June 10, 1897), 741.

58 Thompson, "Poetry of the Civil War," *Chautauquan,* X (February, 1890), 567.

59 Thompson, "Current American Poetry," *Independent,* XLIV (May 19, 1892), 684.

60 Thompson, "The Sapphic Secret," 211.

61 Thompson, "Literary Cant," *Independent,* XLIII (December 31, 1891), 1939.

62 Thompson, "Tomorrow's Poetry," *Independent,* XL (November 1, 1888), 1393.

63 Thompson, "Contemporary American Authors," *Chautauquan,* XXIII (June, 1896), 283.

64 Thompson, "Miss Dickinson's Poems," *America,* V (January 8, 1891), 425.

65 Thompson, "Browning's Place in the Future," *America,* III (December 26, 1889), 407.

66 Thompson, "Literary Reciprocity," *Independent,* XLIV (July 28, 1892), 1041.

67 Thompson, "The American Bouquet," *America,* III (December 12, 1889), 344; Thompson, "Current American Poetry," 684.

68 Thompson, "The Poetry of J. W. Riley," *Critic,* XXXIII (December, 1898), 460.

69 Thompson, "Colors from Keats," *Independent,* XXXVIII (November 18, 1886), 1547.

70 Thompson, "Literary Judgments," *Independent,* LIII (March 14, 1901), 602.

71 Thompson, "In the Matter of Shakespeare," in *Sylvan Secrets,* 58-70.

72 Thompson, "The Lyric Muse," *Independent,* XLV (December 7, 1893), 1642. The following statement, depending on undefined terms and unsupported generalization, is a good index to his method: "All great lyric geniuses have been dramatic, and all great dramatic poets have at need shown a perfect lyric competency. This is the best possible evidence to prove that the lyric and dramatic forms of poetic expression are but different modes of motion generated by the same energy."

73 Thompson, "America's Poet," *Critic*, XIII (December 1, 1888) , 278.
74 Thompson, "Glimpses of Western Farm Life," *Scribner's*, XVI (September, 1878) , 686.
75 Thompson, "Urban Censorship," 739.
76 Hamlin Garland, *Roadside Meetings* (London, 1931) , 104.
77 Thompson, "The Urban Influence," *America*, V (November 27, 1890) , 244; Thompson, "Literary Cant," 1939; Thompson, "The Poetry of J. W. Riley," 46; Thompson, "Literary Half-Acres," *Independent*, XLIV (November 3, 1892) , 1545.
78 Thompson, "Some Notes on Southern Literature," 609; Thompson to R. W. Gilder, November 25, 1886, in Century Collection; Thompson, "Literary Reciprocity," 1041.
79 Thompson, "A Certain Condéscension in Natives," *Independent*, XLII (October 2, 1890) , 1367; Thompson, "Some Plain Words," *Independent*, XLIII (December 3, 1891) , 1783; Thompson, "A Provincial View," *Independent*, XL (November 29, 1883) , 1524; Thompson, "Who Is to Blame?" *Independent*, XLI (July 18, 1889) , 913.
80 Thompson, "Barriers Against Universality," *America*, IV (April 7, 1890) , 75.
81 Thompson, "Literary Loyalty," *America*, II (July 4, 1889) , 421; Thompson, "The Critics and Russian Novels," 1163; Thompson, "Are We a Nation of Thieves?" *Independent*, XLII (July 3, 1890) , 909; Thompson, "The Vote on Copyright," *America*, IV (May 29, 1890) , 243; Thompson, "Foreign Influence on American Fiction," *North American Review*, CXLIX (July, 1889) , 118.
82 See, for example, William Charvat's "Literature as Business," in *Literary History of the United States*, edited by Robert E. Spiller and others (Rev. ed.; New York, 1957) , 961-62.
83 Thompson, "Stranger in Tuscaloosa," *Independent*, LII (May 31, 1900) , 1299; Thompson, "Virility in Fiction," *Independent*, XLIII (May 7, 1891), 673; Thompson, "The Art of Being Provincial," *Independent*, XLVII (August 29, 1895) , 1153.
84 Thompson, "The Provincial Poet," *America*, III (March 20, 1890) , 788; Thompson, "A Stroll in Indiana with a British Critic," *Independent*, XLVII (May 9, 1895) , 616; Thompson, "A Hint to Chicago," *America*, V (November 6, 1890) , 158; Thompson, "Literature and the Exposition," *America*, V (December 11, 1890) , 314.
85 "Gen. Lew Wallace's Tribute to Maurice Thompson," Indianapolis *News*, February 15, 1901; Thompson, "Shall This Thing Be?" *Independent*, LII (August 23, 1900) , 2023-25.
86 Thompson to Howells, June 2, 1881, in Howells Collection; Thompson to R. W. Gilder, November 6, 1886, in Century Collection.
87 Thompson, "Cash Down or Percentage?" *Critic*, IV (February 16, 1884) , 73; Thompson, "Cadmean Bucket-Shops," *America*, V (October 16, 1890) , 73; Thompson, "Poetry and Money," *Independent*, XLIII (October 8, 1891) , 1477; Thompson's address to the Western Association of Writers cited in *Critic*, IX (October 16, 1886) , 187; Thompson, "The Book-Making Disease," *America*, III (February 27, 1890) , 693; Thompson, "Cacoethes Scribendi," *Independent*, XLVIII (September 24, 1896) , 1286.
88 Thompson, *The Ethics of Literary Art*, 55, 63.
89 Thompson, "Christianity and Poverty," *Independent*, LXI (November 7, 1889) , 1458.

90 Thompson, "A Plea for the Rich," *Independent,* XLII (April 17, 1890), 511.

91 Thompson, *Sylvan Secrets,* 30. Thompson often indulged in this kind of equivocation.

92 Howells, *Literature and Life* (New York, 1902), 35.

93 Thompson, "Christianity and Poverty," 1458.

94 Thompson, "A Plea for the Rich," 511.

95 Thompson, "Man on the High-Horse," *Cosmopolitan,* XXVIII (March, 1900), 507-508.

96 Thompson, "The Alien Taint in Criticism," 631; Thompson, "On the Prairie's Edge," 2801.

97 Thompson, "Sentimentality *versus* the Law," *Independent,* XLIII (March 26, 1891), 443.

98 Thompson, *By-Ways and Bird Notes,* 34; Thompson, "The Western Literary Outlook," 278.

99 Thompson, "Glimpses of Western Farm Life," 676.

100 Thompson, "Literary Sincerity," *Independent,* XL (March 8, 1888), 291; Thompson, "Will Imagination Run Dry?" 623; Thompson, "The Domain of Romance," 335.

101 Thompson, "Impressions of the World's Fair," *Critic,* XXIII (November 25, 1893), 334.

102 Thompson, "Pure or Mixed," *Independent,* XLIII (June 11, 1891), 865; Thompson, "The Intellectual Future of the Negro," *Independent,* XLIII (April 16, 1891), 550; Thompson to R. W. Gilder, August 30, 1889, in Century Collection.

103 Thompson, "The Court of Judge Lynch," 254.

104 Thompson, "A Leaf from an Old Book," 171; Thompson, "The Big Bow-Wow," *America,* III (November 14, 1889), 215; Thompson, "Bewildered Critics," *Independent,* LI (November 9, 1899), 3109.

105 Thompson, "The Magnetic Story," *Independent,* LII (June 25, 1900), 241.

106 Thompson's autobiographical novel, *A Banker of Bankersville,* deals with the question. See Chap. 5.

107 Merle Curti, *The Growth of American Thought* (New York, 1943), Chap. 1.

108 Thompson, *My Winter Garden,* 256.

109 Thompson, "Urban Censorship," 739; Thompson, "The Theory of Fiction-Making," 46; Thompson, "Studies of Prominent Novelists: Hawthorne," *Book News,* VI (February, 1888), 261. T. W. Higginson immediately caught the impossible chronology of the last article in a letter to the *Independent:* "A Precursor of Hawthorne," XL (March 29, 1888), 385.

110 Thompson to Howells, October 8, 1883, in Howells Collection; Thompson to R. U. Johnson, February 15, 1900, in Century Collection; regarding the Riley matter, see "The Lounger," *Critic,* XXXIV (March, 1889), 220.

111 Thompson, "A New Edition of Poe's Works," *Independent,* XLVIII (February 13, 1896), 220; Thompson, "Reserve and Understatement," *America,* III (November 28, 1889), 279; Thompson, "The Limit of Criticism," 305; Thompson, "On Being Independent," *Independent,* XLVI (December 27, 1894), 1680.

112 Thompson, *The Ethics of Literary Art,* 9, 23.

113 Grant C. Knight, *James Lane Allen and the Genteel Tradition* (Chapel Hill, N.C., 1935), 65.

114 "Mr. Maurice Thompson on Mr. Howells," *Literary World,* XVIII (Sep-

tember 3, 1887), 281. Other articles in which the controversy may be traced are Thompson's "Two Opinions of Tolstoi," *Literary World,* XVIII (July 23, 1887), 233; "Is Tolstoi a Crank?" *Literary World,* XVIII (August 20, 1887), 264; "Tolstoi," *Literary World,* XVIII, 265; and editorial, *Literary World,* XVIII (September 3, 1887), 280.

115 See George Trumbull Ladd's "Psychology of the Modern Novel," *Andover Review,* XII (August, 1889), 134; Thompson's "Art for Mankind's Sake," *Independent,* XLI (September 12, 1889), 1170; and Ladd's "Ethics of Art," *Independent,* XLI (October 24, 1889), 1374.

116 Thompson, "The Sapphic Secret," 211.

117 Sidney Kramer, *A History of Stone and Kimball* (Chicago, 1940), 49-50.

118 Laura Stedman and George M. Gould, *Life and Letters of Edmund Clarence Stedman* (2 vols.; New York, 1910), II, 262-63; More, "Books and Literature," 1420.

Notes to Chapter IV

1 *Scott's,* VII (January, 1869), 80.

2 Davidson, *Living Writers of the South,* 558.

3 *Dictionary of American Biography,* XVIII, 460; Banta, *Indiana Authors,* 319. Arthur W. Shumaker, in *A History of Indiana Literature* (Indianapolis, 1962), 317, judges Thompson an inferior poet.

4 Thompson, "F. O. Ticknor—Other Poets and 'The Poet,'" *Scott's,* V (February, 1868), 14; Thompson, "Longfellow—Flower-de-Luce," 491.

5 Thompson, "America," in *Poems,* 181.

6 Thompson, "In Captivity," in *Poems,* 1-2.

7 Thompson, "The Ballad of a Little Fun," *Century,* L (June, 1895), 306-307.

8 Thompson, "Independence Day," *America,* VI (July 9, 1891), 428. This Chicago magazine, though short-lived, was one of the loudest organs of nationalism in the Midwest.

9 Thompson, "For Cuba," *Independent,* XLVII (December 5, 1895), 1633.

10 Thompson, "The Lion's Cub," *Independent,* L (December 29, 1898), 1901.

11 Thompson, "The Flagship," *Independent,* LI (April 20, 1899), 1073.

12 Thompson, "A Ballad of Harvest Time," *Independent,* LI (October 5, 1899), 2688.

13 The comparison with Senator Beveridge is taken from the Indianapolis *News,* February 15, 1901.

14 Thompson to R. W. Gilder, August 30 and September 7, 1889, in Century Collection.

15 Thompson, "A Voodoo Prophecy," *Independent,* XLIV (January 21, 1892), 73.

16 Behind this feeling lies the folk belief in the superior potency of the Negro male and, hence, for the white man, the almost intolerable fear of sexual defeat in competition with the Negro. That this fear probably enters into Thompson's attitude signifies only that he was a product of his times.

17 "No man (or king or lord or churl) / Dared whisper love to that fair girl." (*Poems,* 119)

18 Thompson, "To Ceres," *Appleton's,* XI (June 6, 1874), 723. This stanza, incidentally, is highly suggestive of Frost.

19 Thompson to R. W. Gilder, December 6, 1892, in Century Collection.

20 Thompson, "The Golden Pastoral," *Independent,* XLV (September 14, 1893), 1253.

21 Thompson, "Written on a Fly-Leaf of Theocritus," in *Poems,* 126.

22   Thompson, "Between the Poppy and the Rose," in *Poems,* 85-86. This poem was originally published in the *Independent,* XXVI (Ocober 8, 1874), 4, and included in *Songs of Fair Weather.*

23   For example, Emerson's "Waldeinsamkeit," "Woodnotes," and "The Humble Bee."

24   Thompson's "The Fawn" was first published in *Harper's,* LIV (May, 1877), 791, and included in both *Songs of Fair Weather* and *Poems.* "A Prelude" was first published in *Atlantic,* LII (July, 1883), 23, and included in both the later volumes. "The Assault" was first published in *Critic,* XVIII (March 7, 1891), 127, and included in *Poems.* "Spring's Torch-Bearer" was first published in the *Independent,* XLIII (April 30, 1891), 654, and included in *Poems.*

25   Thompson's poem was published seven months before Dickinson's.

26   See Thompson's presidential address at the second annual meeting of the Western Association of Writers, reprinted in *Critic,* IX (October 16, 1886), 187. He also said at other times that the artist should create with no thought of money; but the former attitude played the larger part in his work. The origin and effect of this double standard are discussed in Chap. 3.

27   See *Literary World,* XIV (September 8, 1883), 299; *Dial,* IV (October, 1883); *Harper's,* LXIX (November, 1884), 967; *Independent,* XXXV (October 4, 1883), 1249; *Atlantic,* LII (December, 1883), 841-43; *Nation,* XXXVII (October 18, 1883), 337; *Academy,* XXV (January 26, 1884), 59; *Century,* XXVIII (July, 1884), 466; *Lippincott's,* XXXIII (March, 1884), 319.

28   In letters to Aldrich (February 4, 1884) and to Howells (October 8, 1883) he expressed his appreciation for their kind words in the *Atlantic* and the *Independent,* respectively. These letters are in the Houghton Library, Harvard University.

29   *Atlantic,* LXXII (September, 1893), 416; *Dial,* XII (June, 1892), 54; *Nation,* LIV (March 31, 1892), 253; *Literary World,* XXIII (March 26, 1892), 105; *Literary News,* XIII (April, 1892), 104; *Critic,* XXI (July 9, 1892), 16; *Independent,* XLIV (April 7, 1892), 485.

30   *Critic,* XXV (October 20, 1894), 257; *Independent,* XLVI (July 19, 1894), 931; *Dial,* XVIII (February 1, 1895), 84. See also a publisher's advertisement in *The Chap-book,* II (May, 1894), 490, quoting from the Indianapolis *News.*

Notes to Chapter V

1   Thompson to Gilder, October 25, 1886, in Century Collection.

2   Thompson, "Marvin and His Boy Hunters," *St. Nicholas,* XI (May-October, 1884), 562-67, 645-55, 702-11, 797-806, 879-89, 953-58. It was also included in *The Boys' Book of Sports* (New York, 1886).

3   "Literary Notes," *Independent,* XLIV (November 10, 1892), 1601.

4   Thompson, "The Story of Robin Hood," *St. Nicholas,* X (May-July, 1883), 489-94, 576-80, 655-59.

5   Thompson, "The Mill of God," *Scott's,* VIII (July, 1869), 527. The novel ran serially from February to October, 1869.

6   The characterizations reflect again Thompson's attitude toward sex. The sexual aspect of Monster's origin is emphasized, while Donald is portrayed as a virginal type, completely without interest in the opposite sex.

7   "The Lounger," *Critic,* XV (September 28, 1889), 153.

8   *The King of Honey Island* originally appeared as a serial in the New York *Ledger*, September 3-December 10, 1892. "Banzou Jean" was published in *Lippincott's*, XLIV (October, 1889) , 584-93.

9   *Hoosier Mosaics* (1875) was reprinted in facsimile in 1956 with an introduction by John T. Flanagan, Gainesville, Fla.

10 The sentimental concept was not always characteristic of the New England local colorists.

11 Thompson, *Hoosier Mosaics*, 63. This character, represented in the story "Big Medicine" as a kind of quack doctor, is drawn, according to R. E. Banta of Crawfordsville, from one of his great-uncles, who was actually a graduate of a Cincinnati medical college and quite a cultured man.

12 *Ibid.*, 19-20.

13 Thompson, *Stories of the Cherokee Hills*, 5.

14 Thompson, "A Friend to the Devil," *Lippincott's*, LVI (August, 1895) , 257. This is clearly the best of Thompson's local-color stories. Unaccountably, he left it out of the collected *Stories of the Cherokee Hills*.

15 *Ibid.*, 265.

16 Thompson, "Smithers," *Lippincott's*, XLIX (June, 1892) , 723-34.

17 See the following stories by Thompson which appeared in the *Ledger*: "Mademoiselle Faurie's Choice," XLVII (February 14, 1891) , 14; "Andre the Minstrel," XLVII (January 31, 1891) , 10; "Paul," XLCIII (January 9, 1892) , 14; "The Seal of a Louisiana Feud," XLVII (December 5, 1891) , 1; "A Legend of Bayou Galere," XLVIII (January 16, 1892) , 14; "Bonsoir," XLVII (May 2, 1891) , 14; and "The Lost Count de Lisle," XLVIII (August 6, 1892) , 1.

18 *A Tallahassee Girl* (Boston, 1882) ; *His Second Campaign* (Boston, 1883) ; *At Love's Extremes* (New York, 1885) ; *A Banker of Bankersville; Sweetheart Manette; Rosalynde's Lovers;* "Summer Sweethearts," *Outing*, III-IV (January-July, 1884) .

19 Thompson, *A Banker of Bankersville,* 320.

20 *Ibid.*, 317-18.

21 *Ibid.*, 323.

22 *Ibid.*, 122.

23 *Ibid.*, 158-59.

24 *Ibid.*, 152.

25 See also *A Tallahassee Girl*, in which Cauthorne, the protagonist, is a successful writer of romances, and *Sweetheart Manette*, in which Roland Woodville is a realistic novelist inclining toward anarchism, pessimism, and misanthropy.

26 "Summer Sweethearts" also uses the courtship of a southern heroine by a northern hero, but it occurs at a Hoosier watering place, and sectional contrasts get little attention.

27 Thompson, *His Second Campaign,* 126.

28 Thompson, *At Love's Extremes,* 73.

29 Thompson, "The Lily of Rochon," St. Paul *Pioneer Press*, March 3, 10, 17, 24, 31, 1889.

30 William H. English, *Conquest of the Territory Northwest of the River Ohio* (2 vols.; Indianapolis, 1896) . This book was published by Bowen-Merrill, the same firm that suggested to Thompson the possibilities of a novel on the subject.

31 Despite Thompson's dedicatory note in which he implies that *Alice of Old Vincennes* was based on certain letters written in later years by the

heroine to her step-father, the letters have never been discovered nor has the dedicatee, "M. Placide Valcour, M.D., Ph.D., LL.D." The New York *Times* (February 16, 1901) also asserted that there was historical basis for the love story, but none has ever been discovered. Thompson was very careful in the book never to assert that his lovers are historically verifiable.

32   Thompson, *The King of Honey Island,* 266.

33   Thompson, *Alice of Old Vincennes,* 148-49.

34   *Ibid.,* 189.

35   An interesting circumstance that may also relate to the popularity of the book is that two of Thompson's contemporaries were making novels of this same material when his book appeared. One was Mary Hannah Krout's sister Caroline, who also lived in Crawfordsville. The other is not identified. (See the article on Caroline Krout in Banta, *Indiana Authors and Their Books,* and the sketch of Thompson in *Current Literature,* XXX [April, 1901], 490.) While Thompson was working at a drama on the subject, Lee Burns, an agent of Bowen-Merrill Company, suggested that he write a novel instead. (Burns to Dorothy Russo, March 1, 1950, furnished by Mrs. Russo.) Thus three writers and a publisher had all decided independently that the material would make a good story, so it is not surprising that the public agreed.

36   Thompson, *A Fortnight of Folly* (New York, 1888), 100.

37   *Ibid.,* 26-27.

38   *Ibid.,* 123.

39   *Ibid.,* 77-78, 80.

40   *Ibid.,* 68-69.

41   *Ibid.,* 65. There is no doubt that Thompson's views are those put in the mouth of Peck: he frequently said substantially the same thing in his critical essays, and in one letter to R. W. Gilder, after Gilder had turned down one of his stories, he wrote, "I am sick and tried of trying to please a public taste and to meet an editorial demand which is manufactured in New York and Boston. . . I knew when I last consented to write a story for you that, unless I wrote a dialect something, you wouldn't have it. . . ." Thompson to Gilder, April 19, 1887, in Century Collection.

42   "Hoosier Mosaics," *Independent,* XXVII (September 30, 1875), 9; James I. Osborne, "Maurice Thompson," *Indiana Magazine of History,* XLV (September, 1949), 274; Krout, "Maurice Thompson at Home," 416.

43   See *Literary News,* III (April, 1882), 118; *Harper's,* LXV (June, 1882), 155-56; *Literary World,* XIII (March 25, 1882), 98; *Lippincott's,* XIX (May, 1882), 528; *Nation,* XXIV (May 4, 1882), 385.

44   See *Literary News,* IV (August, 1883), 259; *Literary World,* XIV (July 14, 1883), 228; *Lippincott's,* XXXVI (August, 1883), 231.

45   See *Critic,* VII (July 11, 1885), 17; *Literary World,* XVI (July 25, 1885). 261; *Dial,* IV (September, 1885), 123; *Lippincott's* XXXVI (August, 1885), 216.

46   For *A Banker of Bankersville* see *Literary World,* XVIII (May 28, 1887), 169; *Critic,* X (February 12, 1887), 77. For *The King of Honey Island* see *Literary News,* XIV (April, 1893), 108. For *Stories of the Cherokee Hills* see *Atlantic,* LXXXIII (February, 1899), 287; *Outlook,* LX (October 29 and December 3, 1898), 536, 875. For *Alice of Old Vincennes,* see *Independent,* LII (November 1, 1900), 2635; *Literary News,* XXII (January, 1901), 1; *Bookman,* XII (December, 1900), 348; Jeanette Gilder, "A Western Historical Novel," *Critic,* XXXVII (November, 1900), 406-407.

47 Jeanette Gilder, "A Western Historical Novel," 406-407; letter to writer from Thompson's granddaughter, Mrs. Josephine Ballard Davis, who was a resident of Tallahassee about 1915-20.

48 Letter to writer from D. L. Chambers, president of Bobbs-Merrill Company; Vincennes *Sun-Commercial,* February 18, 1947 (summary furnished by Mrs. Dorothy Russo).

49 "Popular Fiction of 1901," *Bookman,* XIV (January, 1902), 454.

50 Lewis C. Strang (ed.), *Players and Plays of the Last Quarter Century,* (2 vols.; Boston, 1902), II, 242-47. See also Norman Hapgood, "Drama of the Month," *Bookman,* XIV (January, 1902), 527.

51 "The Lounger," *Critic,* XXXVIII (March, 1901), 212. According to the *English Catalogue,* the American edition was on sale in England in November.

52 See Maxwell Geismar, *Rebels and Ancestors* (Boston, 1953), 385; Grant C. Knight, *The Critical Period in American Literature* (Chapel Hill, N.C., 1951), 86-87; Montrose J. Moses, *Literature of the South* (New York, 1910), 411, 412; Fred Lewis Pattee, *History of American Literature Since 1870* (New York, 1915), 433; Van Wyck Brooks, *The Confident Years* (New York, 1952), 147; Alfred Kazin, *On Native Grounds* (New York, 1942), 9.

53 See Edward Wagenknecht, *The Cavalcade of the American Novel* (New York, 1952), 197; Carl Van Doren, *The American Novel* (New York, 1940), 248; Brooks, *The Confident Years,* 69; Arthur H. Quinn, *American Fiction* (New York, 1936), 494 ff.; Ernest E. Leisy, *The American Historical Novel* (Norman, Okla., 1950), 90, 182.

INDEX

161

LOUISIANA STATE UNIVERSITY STUDIES

The Studies was established to publish the results of research by faculty members, staff, and graduate students of the University. Manuscripts of exceptional merit from sources other than aforementioned are considered for publication provided they deal with subjects of particular interest in Louisiana.

The Studies originally appeared as a unified series consisting of forty-two numbers, published between the years 1931 and 1941. In 1951 the Studies was reactivated, and is now being issued in the following series: Social Sciences, Humanities, Biological Sciences, Physical Sciences, and Coastal Studies. Other series may be established as the need arises.

PACIFIC NORTHWEST

BILL YENNE

MALLARD PRESS

Acknowledgments
The author and publisher would like to thank
the following people who helped in the preparation of this book: Don Longabucco, the
designer; Susan Bernstein, the editor, and
Rita Longabucco, the picture editor.

Photo Credits
Amwest: Marv Binegar: 4-5, 25, 28
  (bottom), 50, 56, 57; Bedford Chandler:
  54-55, 67, 73, 75; Bill Everitt: 34;
  Jerry Fields: 51; Mark Newman: 68; Jane
  Palmquist: 20, 32, 66, 96; Robert
  Pritzer: 15; Paul Schaufler: 14, 26-27,
  46, 47, 58-59, 62-63, 65, 69, 70-71,
  78, 79, 80-81, 84-85.
Comstock: 44.
William G. Hartshorn: 6, 8, 11, 12-13,
  18-19, 24, 28 (top), 36, 38-39, 41.
New England Stock Photo: David
  Blankenship: 48, 74; Peter Cole: 30-31,
  60; David E. Rowley: 2, 33.
Photo/Graphics Stock Library, North
  Vancouver, British Columbia: Michael
  E. Burch: 64 (bottom); J.A. Kraulis:
  49, 64 (top).
Chuck Place Photography: 1, 7, 10, 16,
  17, 21, 29, 35, 37, 40(both), 42-43,
  45, 52-53, 61, 72, 76-77, 82, 83,
  86, 87, 88-89, 90, 91 (both), 92-93,
  94-95.
Tourism Vancouver: 22-23.

Page 1: *The Haceta Head Lighthouse at Cape Perpetua on the rugged Oregon coast south of Yachats. The cape, which is part of the Siuslaw National Forest, rises 800 feet above the breakers, making it the highest headland on the Oregon coast.*

Page 2: *A ceremonial mask from Wiseman's Village, British Columbia.*

Below: *South Sisters and Broken Top are reflected in Sparks Lake, Oregon. The three peaks, now referred to generically as "the Sisters," were once known as Faith, Hope and Charity.*

Contents

Introduction

Since the sixteenth century, the notion of the "Northwest" has beckoned to pioneer-spirited Europeans and North Americans. Indeed, the Northwest has always been as much a concept or a state of mind, whose definitions — involving such ideas as an untamed wilderness or a passage to the Pacific Ocean — have always come down to something like the "place at the end of the rainbow."

In the beginning there was the Northwest Passage for which explorers and fur traders searched for centuries. Then there was the "old" Northwest — the wilderness of Michigan and Wisconsin. Today, the Northwest is a slice of rugged coastland running from the states of Washington and Oregon to the Canadian province of British Columbia, and including interior lands to the Cascade Mountains.

Before the Spanish, English and Russian traders of the eighteenth century and before Lewis and Clark's historic expedition in 1805, these lands were home to the Haida, Nootka, Tlingit, Kwakiutl and Chinook Indians, the complexity and sophistication of whose art and architecture was unequaled anywhere in North America north of the Aztec culture of Mesoamerica. They lived in elaborate log houses and sailed inlets of the ocean in massive 65-foot dugout boats.

The white man began arriving in the early nineteenth century to settle in Oregon's rich Willamette Valley, and by 1859, Oregon was an American state. Washington joined the union too, but not until 1889. To the north, British Columbia — once the domain of the Hudson's Bay Company — was a British Crown Colony until 1871, when it became a Canadian province.

The western part of this region is a rugged coastline over which towers the Coastal Mountain Range. Between the Coastal Mountains and the great Cascade Mountain Range there are wide, fertile valleys, such as Oregon's Willamette. Beyond the Cascades, stretching for hundreds of miles to the foothills of the Rocky Mountains, is the Great Basin, a vast, high desert which receives only a tiny fraction of the rainfall that falls along the coast. Pacific storms drop much of their rain on the coastal hills, and the valleys west of the Cascades absorb nearly all that is left over. Nearly, but not all, for the Palouse and Yakima valleys contain exceptionally rich farmlands.

The Pacific Northwest is bisected by two great waterways. First there is Puget Sound and the two channels that connect it with the North Pacific: the Strait of Georgia, which separates Vancouver Island from mainland British Columbia, and the Strait of Juan de Fuca, which separates Canada from the United States.

The second great waterway is the Columbia River — Woody Guthrie called it the King Columbia — which divides Oregon from Washington. The Columbia flows for 1400 miles south from British Columbia through Washington, turning west to form a mile-wide gorge that separates the two Northwest states, reminiscent of — although larger than — Germany's Rhine. The hydroelectric dams on the mighty Columbia generate more electricity than any other hydroelectric project in the world.

The Northwest is a unique place where dormant, glacier-encrusted volcanos rise abruptly above fruitful farmland, where fishing villages continue to thrive as they have for more than a century and where the cities are consistently voted the most livable on the continent.

Left: The office towers of modern Seattle rise above the Alaskan Way waterfront. Once the jumping off point for ships heading north to the Klondike Gold Rush, Seattle's downtown waterfront is now home to numerous tourist attractions, including a world-class aquarium.

Above: Dating from 1856, the Cape Disappointment Lighthouse is the oldest in the Northwest. Located at Fort Canby State Park near the mouth of the Columbia River, it stands guard over one of the most treacherous river bars in the world. As such, it is home to one of the largest search and rescue facilities in the world, housing the Coast Guard's only heavy-weather Motor Lifeboat School.

Northwest Cities and Towns

Most people in the Northwest live in small towns; there are only four cities with populations over 200,000: Vancouver, Victoria, Seattle and Portland.

The state capitals of Olympia and Salem, of Washington and Oregon respectively, have small populations and small town ambience. On the other hand, Victoria, British Columbia's provincial capital, has a small population but exudes world-class charm and sophistication.

"To realize Victoria," Rudyard Kipling wrote, "You must take all that the eye admires in Bournemouth, Torquay, the Isle of Wight, the Happy Valley at Hong Kong . . . Sorrento . . . add reminiscences of the Thousand Islands and arrange the whole around the Bay of Naples, with some Himalayas for the background."

Despite its rugged Northwest setting at the tip of Vancouver Island, Victoria is still quintessentially British, recalling the England of decades past rather than the England of today. It was founded in 1843, and became the capital of all of British Columbia in 1871.

Vancouver, the great port first settled in the 1850s, has been a city since 1886, and is currently Canada's third largest city after Montreal and Toronto. It is western Canada's thriving financial, industrial and cultural capital. Replete with

cosmopolitan charm, it has more ethnic diversity than any other city in the Northwest, and its Chinatown contains the second largest concentration of Chinese people — after San Francisco — in North America.

Seattle, Washington's metropolis, has more skyscrapers than either San Francisco or Los Angeles, and a port that rivals both. Known as the "Emerald City," Seattle was founded in 1851 and named for Seathl, the Indian chief who was paid $16,000 for the land. Reached by the Great Northern Railroad in 1893, Seattle played the role of gateway to the Klondike Gold Rush of 1897, and between 1890 and 1910, its population grew sixfold. Much of the growth of today's modern Seattle began with the 1962 World's Fair, for which the landmark Space Needle was erected. The Boeing Airplane Company, founded here in 1916 and today the world's largest commercial aircraft builder, is Seattle's industrial keystone, although shipbuilding also plays a major role in the financial life of the city.

Portland, Oregon's "City of Roses," was founded in 1845, as Stumptown. A year later, its founders, who hailed from Boston, Massachusetts, and Portland, Maine, flipped a coin to determine which hometown would serve as the namesake for

their new settlement. Portland's strategic location at the confluence of the Willamette and Columbia rivers has served to make it Oregon's commercial hub.

Beyond these few urban centers lie the many small towns and villages of the Northwest Coast — valley farm communities, Cascade Mountain hamlets, resort areas and fishing villages.

Left: Seattle's skyline changed dramatically in the 1980s, but, as we can see in this view from Queen Anne Hill, the Space Needle — built for the 1962 World's Fair — is still the landmark. For over half a century before it was erected, the Smith Tower (the small, pyramid-topped building at the right) was the tallest building on the Seattle skyline. When it was built in 1914, it was the tallest building west of the Mississippi.

Above: Located a stone's throw from Smith Tower, the Pioneer Building is typical of the massive, cast iron architecture in the Pioneer Square district of downtown Seattle. Built in the two decades after the Great Fire of 1889, the 30-square-block Pioneer Square district was Seattle's commercial hub until well after World War II. The modern commercial district, dominated by the skyscrapers (seen left) is immediately to the north of Pioneer Square.

Left: Pioneer Square is a small area located between First Avenue and James Street in the heart of one of Seattle's most historic districts. A statue of Chief Seathl (Seattle) is located here.

Above: A sailboat at rest on Elliot Bay just off downtown Seattle. Elliot Bay, a spur of Puget Sound, is home to practically all of Seattle's saltwater port activities.

Overleaf: Located on Vancouver Island north of Victoria, British Columbia, Butchart Gardens are a dazzling wonderland of floral delights. Azaleas and daffodils burst forth in springtime, while roses and annuals blaze in the warm summer sunshine.

Above: Fireworks over the dome of the State Capitol at Olympia, Washington. Located at the south end of Puget Sound, Olympia has been Washington's capital since the state was admitted to the union on November 11, 1889.

Above: Oregon's State Capitol in Salem, with
its gold-plated statue of an archetypal Oregon
Trail pioneer, was built a half century later
than Washington's more traditional domed
building, although Oregon joined the union
three decades before Washington.

Left: The Jackson House in Jacksonville. Founded in 1852 during the short-lived Oregon Gold Rush, this town's rapid early development came to an end after 1884 when railroad construction bypassed it in favor of Medford. Jacksonville remains a Victorian time capsule, now well-known for its summer music festivals.

Above: The museum and old City Hall in Port Townsend, Washington. Located on the Olympic Peninsula at the mouth of the Puget Sound, Port Townsend's heyday was in the late nineteenth century when it was a strategic trading city, a half day's sail closer to the Orient than Seattle. Port Townsend is best known today for its twice-annual Victorian Homes Tour.

Overleaf: The beautiful Empress Hotel, overlooking Victoria's Inner Harbor, is perhaps the most memorable sight in the capital of British Columbia. The stone-walled Inner Harbor is the heart of the city.

Left: *Stunning Chinese-style long boats on Portland's riverfront. Portland is bisected by the Willamette River, which flows north out of the state's most productive agricultural region, emptying into the mighty Columbia about 10 miles north of downtown.*

Above: *Portland is Oregon's largest city and its commercial hub. Known as the "City of Roses," it hosts an annual Rose Festival. Its remarkably clean central area has earned Portland the reputation of being one of the most livable cities in the United States.*

Overleaf: *A full moon rises over Vancouver, British Columbia's largest city. The pavilions at the left overlooking Vancouver Harbor were part of the World Village built for the popular World's Fair hosted by Vancouver in 1986.*

In the Mountains of the Northwest

Although the Rocky Mountains form British Columbia's eastern border, the mountains of the Northwest can generally be divided into two ranges: the Olympics (the highest range of the Coastal Mountains), which are confined to Washington's Olympic Peninsula, and the Cascades, which follow the coast down through British Columbia, cross both Washington and Oregon and end deep in California at Mount Shasta.

The Cascades are a line of low mountains punctuated by towering, dormant — but not extinct — volcanos. Starting in the north, the major peaks are Mount Baker (10,750 feet), Glacier Peak (10,436 feet), Mount Rainier (14,410 feet), Mount St. Helens (8358 feet), Mount Hood (11,245 feet), Mount Jefferson (10,495 feet) and Mount Shasta (14,162 feet). Mount Hood is the tallest point in Oregon, while Mount Rainier, the highest point in Washington, is also the tallest point in the Cascades.

The most recent volcanic eruption in the Cascade Range occurred at 8:32 AM on May 18, 1980, when a calamitous explosion blew 1313 feet off the top of Mount St. Helens in Washington. It was the first time that volcanic activity had been detected at Mount St. Helens since 1857, and it was the biggest eruption in the continental United States in recorded history. However, it is known that 6850 years earlier, an explosion, hundreds of times more powerful, destroyed Oregon's 12,000-foot Mount Mazama, forming what we now know as Crater Lake.

The Olympic Range is only half as tall as the Cascade Range, but since it rises from sea level rather than tableland, the Olympics appear almost as tall.

Despite the temperate climate of the Northwest, the mountains of the area have numerous permanent glaciers. On Mount Rainier alone there are 26 glaciers covering 34 square miles, and Mount Olympus, in the Olympic Range, has five glaciers.

Left: Towering 14,410 feet above sea level, Washington's ice-clad Mount Rainier is the tallest mountain in the Northwest. Like most major peaks in the Cascade Range, Rainier is a dormant — but not extinct — volcano.

Above: Nutrias, large, beaver-like rodents, basking in the marshes adjacent to Oregon's Molalla River. Oregon is known as the "Beaver State" because trade in beaver pelts — long since discontinued — was once an important part of the state's economy. The beaver is the mascot of Oregon State University in Corvallis.

Overleaf: Mount Rainier at sun-up as seen from Chinook Pass. Dominating this view is the Emmons Glacier, largest of the six glaciers that meet at Rainier's summit.

Above left: *A trio of young Olympic elk cast a watchful eye from a thicket in Olympic National Park. Olympic elk are found only here, and are considered distinct from other North American Elk (Wapiti) subspecies.*

Below left: *A mother moose and her calf. Found throughout the Northwest, moose are the largest members of the deer family. Adult bulls may stand seven feet high at the shoulder and weigh 1400 pounds.*

Above: *A female ruffed grouse. These popular game birds are common throughout the Northwest.*

Overleaf: *A haze-filled view over the Coastal Range in British Columbia.*

Left: What could be more exhilarating than a whitewater canoe trip on the rapids of the upper Willamette River in southern Oregon?

Above: Windsurfing is very popular along the Columbia River.

Above: *The smoldering caldera of Washington's Mount St. Helens. At 8:30 AM on May 18, 1980, St. Helens was a snow-capped jewel among the Cascades standing 9671 feet high. Five minutes later, it was a burning, gray cinder cone standing only 8358 feet above sea level. The incredible explosion that tore the top off this no longer dormant volcano spewed a cloud of smoke and ash 15 miles into the sky, that fell back to earth like a snowstorm, blanketing cities hundreds of miles away with a layer of fine, gray ash.*

Right: *After the Mount St. Helens eruption, thousands of acres of virgin forest were turned into a gray and blackened wasteland. Before long, however, the nutrients present in the volcanic ash soon nurtured a revival of plant life. Beautiful pink fireweed blossoms were among the first to appear as plants reclaimed Mount St. Helens' scarred slopes.*

On the Northwest Coast

It is a temperate, but fog-shrouded land, a mystical land whose heavily wooded hills rise above a labyrinth of coastal waterways. With the cold misty glove of ocean fog hanging in the air, one can look into the warmth of a crackling fire bursting with the wonderful fragrance of big cedar logs and imagine the greatness of the many cultures and people whose fires once burned on these shores.

Before Captain Vancouver and Captain Cook sailed the waters off Cape Perpetua, Cape Foulweather and Cape Disappointment, the Haida, Tlingit, Nootka, Kwakiutl, Chinook and Yaquina Indians lived here, plying the salmon-filled waters much the same way as sportsmen and commercial fishermen do today.

Just like three, or even six, centuries ago, salmon — the silver Coho and the magnificent Chinook — define the economy along the coasts and waterways of the Northwest. All of the major towns on the coasts of the Northwest are fishing and sea-going towns. Port Angeles in Washington and Coos Bay in Oregon are filled with huge ships flying flags from many nations, while countless places field huge fishing fleets.

The Chinook is the king of the salmon, and salmon is king among Northwest seafood, but this delicacy is only part of a story that includes chapters on rock cod, halibut, sea bass and shellfish. The latter includes crab — both Dungeness and Red Rock — as well as shrimp and clams. Oysters, too, are abundant. The southern tip of Puget Sound is home to the unique Olympia Oyster, and Willapa Bay, in Washington's southwest corner, has *two* cities claiming to be "Oyster Capital of the World." Here it is quite common to see piles of discarded oyster shells that are taller than two-story buildings.

The Northwest Coast, steeped in Native American history and bountifully endowed with the fruits of the sea, is truly a marvelous and magical place.

Left and Above: *Completed in 1871, the lighthouse at Yaquina Head near Newport, Oregon, was one of the first of a line of such navigational aids to be built on the Northwest Coast. Once an essential part of life on this hazardous coastline, the Yaquina Head Lighthouse is now a museum with period furnishings. The light, however, still operates.*

Overleaf: *A brilliant, golden sunset over the Pacific.*

Right: *A content and apparently well-fed gull pauses to let his meal digest. Where there are fisherman, there are gulls — well paid for their employment in the art of cleaning fish!*

Overleaf: *Florence, about an hour south of Newport, is situated at the north end of the incredible Oregon Dunes Natural Recreation Area. Mo's is one of a chain of rustic restaurants on the Oregon coast, founded and still operated by Newport resident Mo Neimi and her family. Mo's seafood specialties have been pleasing Oregonians and visitors alike for several decades.*

Above: *Fishing boats at anchor in the harbor at Newport, Oregon. Located in a natural estuary at the mouth of the Yaquina River, Newport's exceptional harbor has helped make it one of the leading commercial and sport-fishing ports on the Oregon coast. Numerous seafood companies line Newport's bay front, packing halibut, crab, shrimp, sea bass and salmon for sale throughout the Northwest. Founded by people from Newport, Rhode Island, this charming, Victorian-era village has also been a popular resort for over a century.*

Right: *A rustic fisherman's cottage at Bandon, Oregon, a small coastal village south of Coos Bay.*

Overleaf: Huge freighters, such as these seen at Olympia, Washington, line up at ports from Coos Bay to Port Angeles to carry Northwest timber to processing plants in the Far East. This book, for example, was probably printed on paper made in Asia from timber cut in the Northwest.

Page 47: A sailor at Port Townsend, Washington, "spinning yarn" — a term for preparing oakum for use as caulking

Above: Like hurling boulders left over from a primordial clash among titans, great stone monoliths, such as these at Face Rock Beach, are a common sight along the Oregon coast between Bandon and Port Orford.

Left: Sunset over the storm-lashed coast of British Columbia.

Above: *A tail of a humpbacked whale off the shores of British Columbia. In the nineteenth century, whaling was a major industry on the Northwest Coast. Since the 1970s, whaling has seen a major comeback, but this time telephoto lenses have replaced harpoons, a fact that can't help but please the whales.*

Right: *Tidal rock pools like this one at Cape Scott, British Columbia, hold small crabs, sea urchins and seaweed as well as many other varieties of marine life.*

Northwest Farmlands

In the early nineteenth century in the days of the Oregon Trail, the lush land of the Northwest valleys, such as Washington's Yakima and Oregon's Willamette, were the pot of gold at the end of the rainbow for thousands of hopeful pioneers. Today, these farmlands are a major component of the economic and cultural backbone of the Pacific Northwest.

The Northwest's most important agricultural product is its timber. British Columbia contains nearly half of Canada's timber reserves, and Oregon has 28 million acres of forest land, more than any other state, except Alaska and California. In fact, Oregon's annual timber production exceeds that of *all* other states, and Washington's timber production ranks second.

In terms of crops, a few statistics are instructive. Washington leads the United States in the production of apples, pears, green peas and sweet cherries. Oregon is second only to Washington in the production of sweet cherries, and leads the nation in growing peppermint, and many types of berries. The highly prized Marion blackberry is indigenous to Oregon's Marion County, and Oregon is second only to California in the production of strawberries. Wheat and hay are also major products in both states, and Washington's Palouse country is the most important wheat-growing region of the area.

It is such a joy to drive the highways and byways of the Northwest and stop at a roadside stand in Wenatchee for a fresh, juicy apple, or near Eugene for a basket of plump berries. The abundant agriculture of the Northwest is just another reason why this region is such a wonderful place to visit — or to live.

Left and Above: Distinctive barns on working farms (*left*) on Washington's Whidby Island and (*above*) in Oregon's Willamette Valley.

Overleaf: A late autumn valley fog creeps into the Willamette. This valley, Oregon's most fertile, is known for dairy farming and orchards.

Pages 54-55: With their golden retrievers as observers, farmers near Waitsburg, Washington, compare the use of horse and mule teams to draw their plows.

Left and Above: Tulip fields near Woodburn, Oregon. Located in the Willamette Valley about 15 miles north of the state capital at Salem, Woodburn is known for its flowers.

Overleaf: The rolling hills of Washington's Palouse River country. Farmers here like to say that they can not only farm the top of their land, but the sides as well! Located south of Spokane near the Palouse River, this area is one of the most important wheat-growing regions in the Northwest.

Left: *A pastoral scene of meadow and meandering stream in British Columbia.*

Above: *A proud bird struts his stuff on the Hovander Homestead near Ferndale, Washington. Located in the northwest corner of the state a few miles from the Canadian border, Ferndale is in the heart of a major agricultural region. The Hovander Homestead is the centerpiece of a large park encompassing a house and barn restored to the way they were in 1903. The Homestead also contains a milkhouse, a children's farm, gardens and picnic areas.*

Overleaf: *Framed by autumn foliage a picturesque farm lies nestled in the rolling hills bisected by Washington's Jackson Highway. Sadly fallen into disrepair, the old barn will not survive too many more winters.*

Page 64 top: *A house sits on the edge of Fraser Canyon, British Columbia.*

Page 64 bottom: *Apple trees bloom in the orchards near Keremeos in southern British Columbia.*

Page 65: *A hop field in Washington's Yakima Valley. One of the last major hop-growing regions in the United States, or indeed in North America, Yakima produces a variety of hops prized by brewers around the world. Yakima's Cascade hops are noted for their distinctive aroma and the crisp fruitiness that they impart to a good beer.*

Left: *A stand of spruce trees tops a hill in Oregon's Lane County. One of western Oregon's two largest counties, Lane spans several ecosystems, from the cool and rugged Pacific Coast to the lush Willamette Valley, and across the Cascade Mountains to the parched basin country west of Bend. The county seat is Eugene, Oregon's second largest city and home of the University of Oregon.*

Above: *An abandoned barn in the hills of Washington's Palouse country. The area between the "Tri-Cities" (Richland/ Kennewick/Pasco) and Pullman contains some of the most productive wheat-growing land in the Northwest. Farmers also grow a lot of alfalfa here.*

Northwest Parklands

Aside from the Canadian national parks in the Rocky Mountains, most of which are shared with the province of Alberta, there are five national parks in the Northwest. These are the Pacific Rim National Park on British Columbia's Vancouver Island, Crater Lake National Park in Oregon and three in Washington: Mount Rainier, North Cascades and Olympic.

Olympic National Park, established in its present form in 1938, contains nearly one million acres and is the largest, while North Cascades National Park, established in 1968, is the newest. The US National Park Service also has jurisdiction over the Oregon Dunes National Recreation Area on the Pacific Coast and Hells Canyon National Recreation Area on the Oregon border with Idaho.

The US Forest Service also administers about one-third of the land in both Washington and Oregon in the form of national forests. These include the Snoqualmie,

Wenatchee, Okanogan and Gifford Pinchot National Forests in Washington and the Mount Hood, Rogue River and Umpqua National Forests in Oregon. On the Oregon coast, about a third of the coastal mountain range and parts of the coast itself are included in the Siuslaw National Forest.

British Columbia has 10 large provincial parks. Most are in the northern part of the province, but the Garibaldi Provincial Park is immediately outside the city of Vancouver. Washington has many small state parks, with over half of them around, or on an island in, the Puget Sound. Oregon also has an unexcelled system of coastal state parks that averages one every 19 miles — from the Columbia River to the California border.

Facilities at the parks vary, but most provide overnight camping, and all afford an opportunity to experience a unique slice of the Northwest in a nearly natural state.

Left: Crater Lake in southwest Oregon is a remarkable place. An enormous volcanic explosion 6850 years ago, created the crater that is 26 miles around. The brilliant blue lake that fills it is 1932 feet deep.

Above: A cross-country skier on the slopes of Mount Rainier in Washington. With 25 glaciers, most of Mount Rainier and its foothills are always white.

Overleaf: Upper Royal Basin in Olympic National Park. Located on the Olympic Peninsula, the park contains glaciers that are within 40 miles of the Pacific Ocean.

Left: Early morning light filtering through the massive cedars at Soleduck Falls in the northwest corner of Olympic National Park. The park preserves some of the only surviving rain forests in the continental United States.

Above: Silver-trunked aspen in autumn cloaks amid the basalt boulders in northeast Oregon's Eagle Cap Wilderness Area.

Above: The sun sets over Pacific Rim National Park, which is located on Vancouver Island's rugged west coast.

Right: Carved from solid granite by ancient glaciers, Ice Lake lies high in the rugged alpine splendor of the Eagle Cap Wilderness Area in northeast Oregon's Wallowa Mountains.

Overleaf: A wonderland of alpine flora carpets the hillsides of Olympic National Park. The red flowers are known as Indian paintbrush, although Native Americans probably never use them as such. The Olympic Mountain Range contains eight glaciers and four peaks over 7000 feet. The tallest is Mount Olympus at 7965 feet. Because the lowlands of the park are nearly at sea level, the Olympic Mountains rise higher from the valley floors than the Colorado Rockies.

Above: Better safe than sorry. This backpacker crossing the Enchantment Lakes Outlet in Washington's Alpine Lakes Wilderness Area could have chosen to walk this log, but it looks pretty rain slicked and slippery.

Above: A hiker pauses to consider the view at Porcupine Creek on the Pacific Crest Trail in North Cascades National Park, Washington's newest national park. The Pacific Crest Trail extends over a thousand miles through three states.

Overleaf: Shi Shi Beach at Cape of the Arches in Olympic National Park near the northernmost point on the Pacific Coast of the continental United States. In addition to its 923,000 acres in the Olympic Range, the park governs a separate 57-mile strip of unspoiled coastline that stretches from Queets to the Makah Indian Reservation at the northwestern tip of Washington. Only about a quarter of this coastal strip is accessible by paved road.

Above: The pounding surf at Shore Acres
State Park in Oregon. The Oregon state park
system contains no fewer than 34 coastal
parks in its 560 miles of coastline, a higher
average than any other coastal state. Most of
these state parks have overnight camping.

Right: A fisherman on the mist-shrouded
beach at Olympic National Park. Salmon are
plentiful here and have been a staple in the
diets of the Quinault and Makah Indians for
centuries.

Overleaf: Ocean mist creeps in to cover the
sand drifts at the Oregon Dunes National
Recreational Area. This area encompasses an
amazing 40-mile stretch of dunes that runs
from Coos Bay to Florence, Oregon. In some
places, the dunes are over two miles wide and
encroach on Highway 101.

Images of
the Northwest

What is the Northwest? A lighthouse on a rocky crag? A Victorian fishing village unchanged in a century? A deep, dark and still rain forest, where the only sound is the dripping of dew from the boughs of centuries-old cedar? A massive, sleeping volcano with 26 glaciers? A bustling cosmopolitan city?

The Northwest is many things to many people. To the pioneers on the Oregon Trail, it was the Promised Land. To sport fishermen, it is Valhalla. To the world's airlines, it is the place where most of the world's jetliners are made. To photographers and tourists, it is a wonderland of stunning vistas, vivid sunsets and unique

natural features, that range from Crater Lake to Mount St. Helens and the strange, rocky monoliths on the coastline.

The Northwest is a visit to Seattle's lively Pike Place Market. The Northwest is a stroll along Newport, Oregon's bay front. The Northwest is a lungful of cool, clean air from high on Mount Rainier. The Northwest is the seven-mile drive across the mouth of the Columbia River. The Northwest is confronting a 50-foot Nootka totem pole standing peacefully in the mist on Vancouver Island.

The Northwest is indeed many things, but most of all, it is a wondrous and magical place.

Left: A rosebush at the Rothschild House in Port Townsend, Washington. The old City Hall can be seen in the background. Dating from the nineteenth century, the Rothschild House is one of the stops on the twice-annual Victorian Homes Tour.

Above: A view from the house built in 1869 by Tom Crellin in Oysterville, Washington. Located at the tip of the Long Beach Peninsula, Oysterville became a boom town after the discovery in 1854 that Willapa Bay (background) is one of the world's richest oyster beds. In the 1860s, an oyster from here could be routinely expected to fetch $50 in gold in San Francisco.

Overleaf: A metal egret, forever poised above the carp at the Japanese garden at Shore Acres State Park in Oregon.

Above: *A killer whale totem at the Burke Museum of the University of Washington in Seattle. The Indian tribes of the Northwest Coast, such as the Haida and Tlingit, had an extraordinarily highly developed art tradition that reached its apogee in their carvings of totem animals, notably on their totem poles.*

Above right: *Crab nets piled high at Winchester Bay, Oregon. The coastal waters of Oregon are rich in both Dungeness and Red Rock Crabs.*

Below right: *A re-creation of a nineteenth century shop at the Linn County Museum in Brownsville, Oregon.*

Overleaf: *Spools of wool at the Thomas Kay Woolen Mill Museum in Salem, Oregon. Completely restored and operating with a water-powered turbine, the 1889 woolen mill demonstrates the process of converting wool fleece into woolen fabric.*

Pages 94-95: *Like images from an impressionist painting, flowers peek through a fence at the Shelburne Inn in Seaview, Washington.*

Page 96: *Back where the book began, this twilight view of the Haceta Head Lighthouse looks back toward the cliffs from which the picture on page 1 was taken. Still operating, the Haceta Head Lighthouse uses Oregon's most powerful beacon.*